W0037870

This special edition is dedicated to Colonel Powell and Captain Hillyer, the officers who left these remarkable memoirs.

They did not know one another, but their lives are inextricably linked forever.

Original dedication to
Captain Hillyer's "My Gettysburg Battle Experiences":

To the memory of Private Ezekiel Parrish and Corporal Isaiah Parrish of Bullock County, who served in Company I, 9th Georgia Infantry, C.S.A.

They fought with Captain Hillyer, and are my ancestors through the lineage of my mother, Lucy Parrish Coco, whose great-great grandfather was Henry Parrish, a sergeant in the 2nd Virginia Infantry during the Revolutionary War.

THE
GREGORY A. COCO
COLLECTION

by Savas Beatie

Two Confederate Officers Remember GETTYSBURG

"The Recollections of
a Texas Colonel at Gettysburg,"
by Col. Robert M. Powell, 4th Texas Infantry, C.S.A

&

"My Gettysburg Battle Experiences,"
by Capt. George Hillyer, 9th Georgia Infantry, C.S.A.

Edited by
Gregory A. Coco

Savas Beatie
California

© 1990, 2005, 2022 Gregory A. Coco
New Materials Copyright 2022 Savas Beatie

Two Confederate Officers Remember Gettysburg

All rights reserved. No part of this publication may be reproduced, stored in a retrieval system, or transmitted, in any form or by any means, electronic, mechanical, photocopying, recording, or otherwise, without the prior written permission of the publisher.

Originally published separately by Thomas Publications in 1990 (Powell) and 2005 (Hillyer).

Library of Congress Control Number: 2022939203

First Savas Beatie Edition, First Printing

ISBN-13: 978-1-61121-647-9
eISBN: 978-1-954547-49-0 (Savas Publishing)

SB

Savas Beatie
989 Governor Drive, Suite 102
El Dorado Hills, CA 95762
916-941-6896
www.savasbeatie.com
sales@savasbeatie.com

Savas Beatie titles are available at special discounts for bulk purchases by corporations, institutions, and others. For more details, please contact contact us at sales@savasbeatie.com or visit www.savasbeatie.com for more information.

TABLE OF CONTENTS

PART I

"The Recollections of a Texas Colonel at Gettysburg,"
by Col. Robert M. Powell, 4th Texas Infantry, C.S.A

PART II

"My Gettysburg Battlefield Experiences,"
by Capt. George Hillyer, 9th Georgia Infantry, C.S.A.

PART I

"The Recollections of a Texas Colonel at Gettysburg,"
by Col. Robert M. Powell, 4th Texas Infantry, C.S.A

Photo Credits:

Adams County Historical Society: p. 28

Gettysburg National Military Park: pp. 11, 17 & 25

Library of Congress: pp. 22, 32

J.B. Polley, Hood's Texas Brigade: pp. 5 & 43

U.S. Army Military History Institute: pp. 8, 10 & 32

All other photos by Gregory A. Coco.

INTRODUCTION

On Saturday, December 13, 1884, an article appeared in the Philadelphia *Weekly Times* entitled "With Hood at Gettysburg."[1] Written by an ex-Confederate officer then living in St. Louis, Missouri, it was probably perused by the general public during that week shortly before Christmas and then quickly forgotten. And oddly enough, the author of this fascinating piece, attorney Robert M. Powell, apparently never again wrote anything else concerning his experiences in the American Civil War. For some unknown reason, twenty-one years and six months after what was likely the supreme moment of his life, Powell felt compelled to transcribe only his experiences during and shortly after the Battle of Gettysburg. These interesting recollections of Colonel Powell, now newly edited and presented in a fresh format and under a different title, are here made available to those readers intrigued by the story of that great contest of arms.

My interest in republishing this article came almost as soon as I read it for the first time. I found this obscure reminiscence while conducting research for a book on the field hospitals and wounded of the Battle of Gettysburg, and immediately realized it was an excellent source for my book. Later, with the encouragement of publisher Dean S. Thomas, the project to reintroduce Powell's memoir to the public began to take shape. The final product is now before you, and we both hope it adds much to your enjoyment of history.

Robert Michael Powell was born in Montgomery County, Alabama in 1826. At the age of 23 he moved to Texas where he was soon engaged in the practice of law. During most of the ten years prior to the War Between the States, Powell lived at Danville, in Montgomery County, Texas, making his living as an attorney and state legislator.[2]

On August 2, 1861, four months after the war began, Robert Powell was commissioned captain of a company of volunteers at Harrisburg, Texas,[3] a rank he held for one year. Most of the enlisted members of his company were recruited from the counties of Walker and Montgomery in July of that year. The regiment itself was assembled at Richmond, Virginia, in October, 1861,[4] with Powell's Company "D" arriving under the nickname of the "Waverly Confederates."[5]

The trip to Virginia, after the companies had been mustered into Confederate service as the 5th Texas Infantry, was quite long and difficult. One veteran of the 5th, W.A. Nabours of Tuscola, Texas recalled his journey to the northeast.

> (After being issued tents and other necessary camp supplies) we could not get to New Orleans by steamer [as the port of Galveston was

blockaded by U.S. war vessels] so we had to take the land route from [Harrisburg] to Beaumont, walking most of the distance, thence to Niblett's Bluff, La., by steamboat. From there our only means of transportation were Creole carts, which we had to force into service. The natives hid their oxen and avoided us in every way possible. But we finally got together enough carts to carry our baggage, and we followed on foot through a low, flat country of pine woods and marshes, sometimes wading in water from four inches to waist-deep all day, and it was difficult to find a place above water to make our beds at night. It was then that the hardships of a soldier's life began for us. On to Lake Charles, New Iberia, and Lafayette, where we met some wealthy French who were kind and wished us Godspeed. From Berwicks Bay to New Orleans we went by railroad, and from there to Grand Junction, Chattanooga, Knoxville, Bristol, Lynchburg, and Richmond, which we reached without the loss of a man. This good fortune was not to continue, however; for sickness began at once, and our boys died at a frightful rate.

We were soon quartered at Camp Bragg, on the York River Railroad, and began active drill service, thus learning some of the demands that would be made on us by our superior officers. In a short time we were organized into a regiment known as the 5th Texas Volunteer Infantry. The colonel appointed was not liked at first appearance, and soon after his arrival in camp his horse's mane and tail were shaved off close. The colonel declined to continue command, so Col. J.J. Archer was appointed to command the 5th Texas and soon went with us to the front on the Potomac near Dumfries, Va., and into winter quarters.[6]

When the winter was over, the Fifth began its hard service and military campaigning which would not end until April of 1865. The regiment was first engaged at Yorktown and Seven Pines, and later it was sent to the Shenandoah Valley to serve for a while under General T.J. Jackson, then back to Richmond and into the battle of Gaines' Mill and several other minor engagements during the Seven Days' Battles. Present at the Second Battle of Manassas,[7] South Mountain and Antietam, the 5th Texas next took a minor part in actions at Fredericksburg and Chancellorsville. Soon afterwards, the regiment was ordered to Suffolk, Virginia where it was involved in skirmishing, sharpshooting, and pickett duty, until it retired to Richmond and then to Orange Court House where it remained until the march into Pennsylvania. During the long months from October 1861 to June 1863 Captain Powell had risen steadily but quickly through the ranks. He was promoted to major on August 22, 1862, lieutenant colonel eight days later, and finally to the rank of colonel on November 1, 1862.[8] At the onset of the Gettysburg Campaign, Powell's regiment consisted of 409 officers and men, of which he would soon lose 54 killed or mortally wounded, 112 wounded, and 97 prisoners

4

and missing. The total: 211.[9]

His narrative will now begin in early June 1863. Colonel Powell quickly takes the reader into the Battle of Gettysburg where the bitter fight of July 2 and the aftermath is viewed through his eyes only. These experiences do not give you the "big picture" of strategy and grand movements but just that of a single soldier witnessing the memorable sights and scenes around him. I believe the strength of this story lies in that very aspect. So it is with great pleasure that after 100 years have passed, here are once more the recollections of a Texas colonel at Gettysburg.

Gregory A. Coco
April 2, 1990

Colonel R.M. Powell
Fifth Texas Regiment

"RECOLLECTIONS"

by

Colonel Robert M. Powell
5th Texas Infantry

On The March.

On the 28th of May marching orders were received with joy by some and with satisfaction by all. The march was slow and tedious. As we moved away from Richmond the counter movements of our adversary grew in importance. Would Hooker uncover Washington to capture Richmond? But the absence of any symptoms of a fixed purpose in that quarter assured General Lee that he need have no fears of his adversary. Outside of a little amusement enjoyed almost entirely by the cavalry at Culpepper and a few other points the march was unembarrassed and uninterrupted by the enemy,[1] and on the 27th of June Longstreet's command crossed the Potomac river at Williamsport. The men waded in water up to their arm-pits, holding their guns and accoutrements above their heads. We went into camp and it was raining and we were wet. Whisky was issued, the first and only time I ever knew it done in the Confederate army. It was better than Virginia "apple jack." The delirious fumes of coffee and frying bacon were an earnest of the good things in this land of plenty. Poor beef and sour flour were henceforth to be only memories of the past.

Signs of Prosperity.

We saw on every side white cottages embowered in groves of trees laden with fruit, around which spread out fields of wheat like restless seas of emerald. The evidences of prosperity, happiness and comfort were in the striking contrast to the dismal, mourning, half peopled land we had just left just over the river. The teeming population leisurely pursuing their occupations, although Mr. Lincoln had called on Pennsylvania for 120,000 militia, was a revelation to us. We had been under the delusion that the enlistment of men in the Union army had affected the population North as it had in the South.[2]

After a few hours rest the march was resumed. The clouds had disappeared and the sun gave a cheerful brightness to this lovely region. Cattle, horses and sheep fed lazily in the meadows. Geese, turkeys, ducks and chickens, leading their young broods met us in the lanes. Pigeons cooed and fluttered about the barns, all innocent of the ways and proverial foraging properties of the soldier. Here were no perceptible evidences of the desolating touch of war, or that its alarms had ever blanched the cheeks or wrung the hearts of waiting wives and mothers. While talking with an old citizen he said that the people had made large outlays of money in the way of bounties to secure volunteers to represent their families in the ar-

General James Longstreet, 42 year old commander of Lee's First Army Corps.

my, but they had been abundantly compensated by the enhanced value of their products.

The First Night.

Before night there seemed to be a large increase of field officers in the army, or the army was changing from infantry to cavalry. The bare-footed and sore-footed had secured horses. Some horses bore three men. We were all very jolly that afternoon. That night an old housewife, with whom General Hood had taken rooms, complained of disturbances among her chickens, and he said: "My dear Mrs. Kountz, my people have seen no chickens for a long time. They are very fond of them." This first night on the enemy's soil was full of interest and incidents. Every company was augmented by the arrival of stragglers and by a class of soldiers known as hospital bummers. [3]

The plans and purposes of the campaign were kept secret until the inward march was resumed. After driving the enemy from Winchester and beyond the river from Culpepper Court House disclosed the fact that we were bound for the enemy's territory. Then there was a hasty and voluntary exodus from hospitals and comfortable retreats and hurrying after the army. Thousands came without organization or preparation, without guns, blankets or rations. Any member of the Army of Northern Virginia who

8

was absent on the day of battle would be ever after disgraced and despised by the comrades.[4] Throughout the night the challenge of sentries was heard and uproarious greetings accorded to each limping laggard. Farmers stood guard over their belongings while the soldiers appointed to that duty were enjoying the hospitalities of unwilling hosts or exercising their persuasive arts to mullify the resentments of the fair sex, who, with unbridled tongue, made things warm.

Lee's Orders.

The next morning special orders from General Lee were read requiring every man to keep his place in the ranks, forbidding any interference with peacable citizens or disturbing private property. We all understood when "Massa Robert" issued an order it meant, "You must and shall obey." Many citizens came forward to claim their horses, which the boys had borrowed the day before. On reaching the camp that night the horses were formally liberated, after being gravely informed "that their manacles had been broken and the burden lifted from their galled withers."

The march was resumed. It is possible that a little butter, milk and "apple sass" lying around loose about spring houses might have been appropriated, but no more horses were "led out of bondage," and spring lamb chickens were as sacred as the idols of the Hindoos.[5]

A Town of Banners.

The march through Chambersburg[6] was the occasion of the usual fun and amusement which a soldier has the genius to discover or create in all situations. This had the appearance of a city of banners. A Union flag surrounded every house, pole and post. Every lady held a flag in her hand, varying in size from a postage stamp to a table cloth. The ragged Confederates pretended to think that each lady intended to distinguish her knight by presentation of her colors. This honor they unanimously declined, declaring that they had taken all the flags they wanted from the Yankee army. When a citizen wearing a desirable hat approached too near the lines he was certain to make an exchange and receive one in return, which had no value except for its antiquity, honorable scars or as a fragmentary relic, mournfully suggestive of the decaying nature of a soldier's crown of glory.

Just Before The Battle.

While the troops were enjoying this novel situation of being in an enemy's country, without seeing an armed foe, charged with the duty of protecting everything animate or inanimate in the line of its promenade, the General was filled with anxiety and perplexity. Stuart, commanding the eyes and ears of the army and who had been sent out to hear and see, had failed to report to his chief.[7] The whereabouts and movements of the Federal army were unknown. On the 28th A.P. Hill was moving towards Gettysburg and Ewell ordered to stay his march on Harrisburg. On the 1st of July Hill's advance encountered the enemy at Gettysburg, and the two armies were

9

Kentuckian John Bell Hood. His association with the Texas and Arkansas troops in the Army of Northern Virginia would give him everlasting fame.

about to confront each other. The guns of Hill called Gordon, who was soon thundering on his left, and the whole Confederate army quickened to participate in the impending struggle.[8]

Orators, writers and glowing canvass have described and illustrated this, the grandest of battles. This paper is only intended to describe and recite the unwritten incidents which only have interest as a part of the great conflict—the pathetic, comic and ludicrous, which play their little parts even when kingdoms are the stakes, and have no place on the stage when heroes are the actors and the world constitutes the audience. This is only a narration of what I saw and a part of which I was.

The March To The Field.

Longstreet's command had just gone out on dress parade a little before sundown on the afternoon of the 1st of July, when orders were received to march immediately. Every man was in his marching and fighting attire and as quickly as the order could be given, "right face, forward, march!" we were on the way to the general meeting of the armies. There was not so much hilarity as usual on this night's march; an occasional report of a bushwhacker's rifle[9], the rattling and jarring of artillery and the measured tramp of infantry were the only sounds presaging the purposes of to-morrow. At 4 o'clock A.M. we halted for rest and to close up the ranks. At daylight we were again in motion. We had reached the scene of the first day's conflict, and the melancholy evidences of its results were not calculated to evoke cheerful reflections or give assurance to those about to participate in the same kind of an entertainment. To the right and to the left among the wounded and dead we recognized comrades with whom we had exchanged greetings two days before. By 7 o'clock we had reached a point from which could be seen the field, already quick with events which were to give it historical interest and value when the actors were forgotten. Coming over the mountains, moving along the valleys, deploying on the plains with flying banners and glittering arms, music calling from every crest and hilltop an echo to swell the chorus, was the grand pageant of gathering armies.

Up The Little Round Top.

About 4 o'clock P.M. on the 2d of July, the preparations were complete. The decision had been made to deliver battle. Staff officers were riding in hot haste to the commanders of divisions and brigades, bearing the compliments of the General and with courteous salute delivering orders to at-

Medical doctor Jerome Bonapart Robertson would begin his military career fighting for the Texas Republic. Renowned as an Indian fighter, he later became a captain in the 5th Texas Infantry.

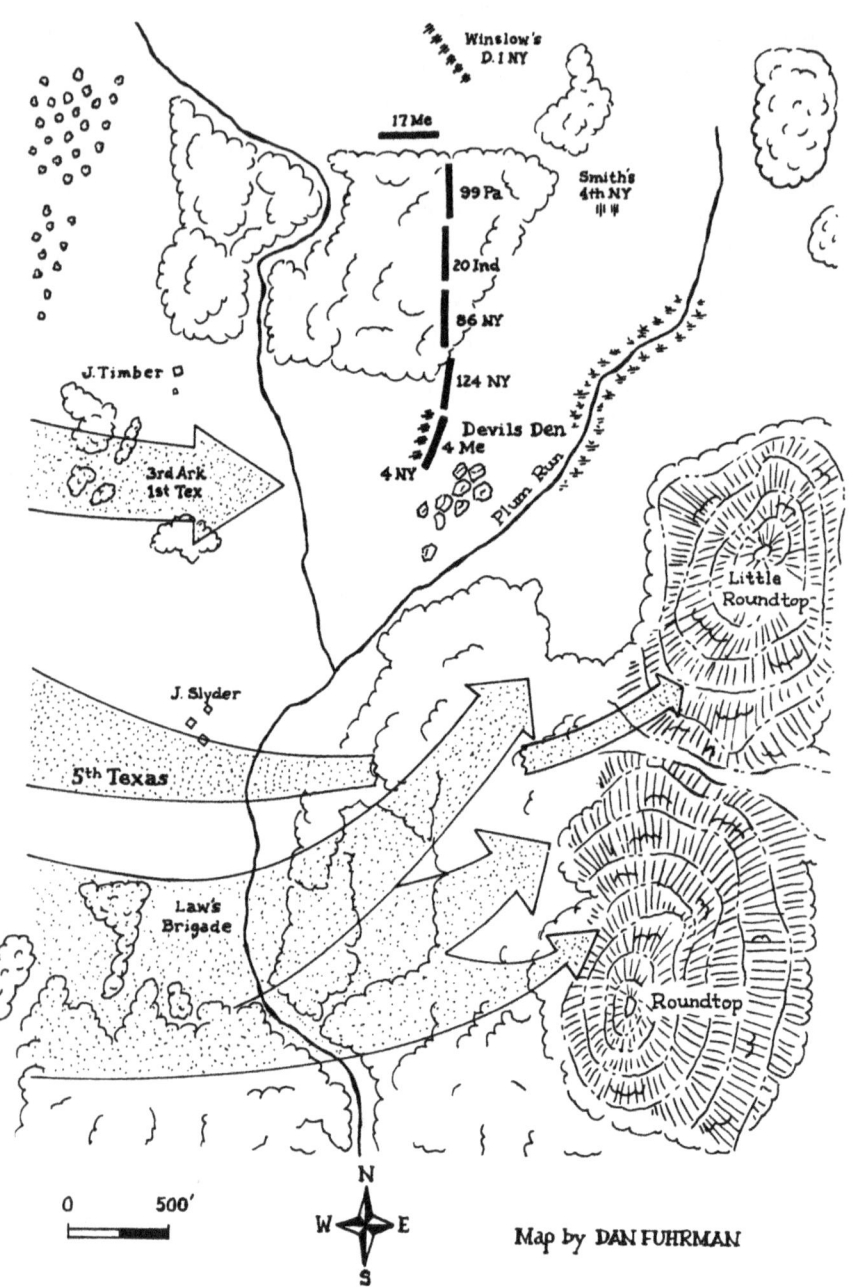

Winslow's
D. 1 NY

17 Me

99 Pa

20 Ind

86 NY

124 NY

Smith's
4th NY

Devils Den
4 Me

4 NY

Plum Run

J. Timber

3rd Ark
1st Tex

J. Slyder

5th Texas

Law's
Brigade

Little
Roundtop

Roundtop

0   500'

N
W   E
S

Map by DAN FUHRMAN

12

General Robertson's brigade's initial position on Warfield Ridge with the Michael Bushman farm to the right in front of Big Round Top.

John Slyder's 80-acre farm west of Big Round Top was traversed by Powell's Texans late on July 2, 1863.

The "gorge" was just east of Houck's Ridge and the Devil's Den. Colonel Powell's left companies may have skirted this area during their attack on Little Round Top.

tack the enemy at the signal. Captain Gorce,[10] of Longstreet's staff, after communicating orders to General Hood, rode down the line and remarked that the possession of Little Round Top—pointing to its rugged heights—was necessary. The Texans were expected to take it.

"We'll do it!" was the reply.

The signal was given and a sheet of flame sprang along the enemy's lines, hurling defiance at the advancing Confederates. Smoke from either side rolled in billows, meeting and writhing in conflict in the valley midway the engaging armies. Soon the artillery duel ceased and rattling musketry announced that the serious work had begun.

Up The Rocky Slope.

On rushed the Texans, sweeping from their path cavalry which met them on the Emmitsburg pike, on through the "Devil's Den,"[11] blazing with infernal fire, crushing and destroying opposing forces at the foot of the mountain, onward and upward they struggled over precipitaous rocks, where the enemy, lying in ambush, was surprised. The ascent was so difficult as to forbid the use of arms. At last, weary and almost exhausted, we reached the topmost defenses of the enemy. Now the conflict raged with wild ferocity. We were caught in a cul de sac or depressed basin, surrounded on three sides by projecting or shelving rocks surmounted by a stone fence. Captain Cleveland, with a voice heard above the din of battle, offered a purse

14

Little Round Top, the "slaughter pen," and Plum Run from Houck's Ridge, much as it looked when the 5th Texas debouched from the woods on the right over 127 years ago.

"...the ground [was] covered with large boulders from the size of a wash pot to that of a wagon bed...." John W. Stevens 5th Texas

to the first man over the works. Sergeant Ross sprang forward to earn the reward when Cleveland ordered him back to his post, remarking: "File closers not included."

"Swing up the left, Major Rogers." [12]

"I'll do it, Colonel, by jingo."

Just at the moment of these utterances there was a sudden cessation of firing, and the last words, "by jingo" were distinct and sounded so ludicrous as to excite laughter.

A Devil's Carnival.

The scene was strikingly like a devil's carnival. Another yell and desperate charge followed, succeeded by a sudden and an awful hush, just as if every one had been stricken instantly with death. I raised my head from the ground, where I lay prostrated by a wound. The only moving man I saw was Sergeant Ross. He leisurely approached the enemy's lines and taking his ramrod, which had been left leaning against a rock, he walked deliberately to the rear. I could see men lying around in every direction and in all attitudes. This desolate silence continued at least thirty minutes; to me it seemed like thirty hours. The twilight was fading into night before the victors came to gather spoils and take charge of the wounded. To their regret the wounded were the only ones who had crossed the enemy's works.

In Union Clutches.

The slightly wounded were the most earnest in their appeals to be left to die where they lay, insisted that it was wanton cruelty to subject dying men to the unnecessary torture of removal and so on. They hoped to be able to escape under cover of darkness and be ready to fight another day. When first taken over the lines I was temporarily placed near a Captain White,[13] a Union officer, posted in our front. During the fight he had held a flag near or on the works and one of the Texans seeing him determined to have that flag. He got it, but the Captain held on to the staff although he seemed to be stuck full of holes by a bayonet; his hands and arms were literally torn to pieces. I think he was the maddest man I ever saw and said he would have given a hundred lives rather than have lost that flag. The Captain and myself were informed by the surgeon that we were mortally wounded. We have met since and fought that battle o'er.

The wounded prisoners were gathered together in the rear of the Federal lines and spread out on the ground in an open field. There we lay, forlorn, wretched, ragged and battered, shivering in the rain. We, however, were critically observant of all of our surroundings. We had an agreeable visit from some cavalry officers. A colonel who said he was from Rochester, N.Y., and was known as "Dare-Devil Dick," gave us substantial and invigorating comfort which he carried in a flask. I have forgotten his name but not his kindness.[14]

Brothers As Foes.

The recognition of two brothers was a circumstance of greater surprise than pleasure—one a staff officer in the Union army and the other a wounded Confederate. Following the national custom of our Yankee brothers the loyal brother essayed a little speech of censure and reproach, which the Confederate promptly discouraged by saying with emphasis that he was competant to decide and act for himself; that inclination and conviction determined his action, and said, however, that he did not believe that actual war would result, thinking the North would willingly permit the South to withdraw from the Union peaceably, as she was not esteemed worthy of a place and part in the national household. "Colonel Dare-Devil Dick" interrupted the controversy by saying "it was not the time or place for such talk." He led his party off in the darkness and left us to meditate upon the eventual fate of a people of one lineage, drawing inspiration from the same traditions, thus divided by the accident of their local habitations.

Colonel Joshua L. Chamberlain, then 44 years old, was one of the first Union soldiers to stumble across the wounded body of Robert Powell among the confusion of boulders near Little Round Top.

17

Talk With Regulars.

We were visited by several members of the Fourteenth United States Regulars,[15] whom we had met on our bloody excursion up Little Round Top. They said we had almost destroyed them. They were Georgians, so they said, and like hundreds of other young fellows had fallen into disgrace at home, had enlisted in the army just before the war. They said they did not take any stock in patriotism or glory, but being in on that side they proposed to stay. I remarked that there seemed to be a good deal of confusion and disturbance among their people. They replied there was great dissatisfaction. The army was worn out by forced marches and were without provisions and very much disheartened by the results of two days' fighting, and thought some other general would do better than Meade. They said it was reported that some of the troops had actually thrown down their arms, and rumors were rife that General Meade intended to retreat before daylight.[16]

A Hurrah For McClellan.

Officers were busy riding among the troops, persuading and commanding. Finally another soldier from the Fourteenth United States Regulars joined our party, and said it was understood that General McClellan would arrive early in the morning with forty thousand troops and would take command of the army![17] This news was received along the lines with a loud "hip, hip, hurrah!" The noise and confusion subsided and the morning dawned upon an army prepared for another conflict. It was easy to discover that the belief of McClellan's presence was worth forty thousand men. His name was a power which General Lee, with his army, could not destroy.

Battle Pictures.

In anticipation of a renewal of the battle we obtained permission to shelter ourselves from the artillery of our own people among some large rocks near a stone house, occupied by an aged German and his wife![18] Everything was quiet during the morning hours. Wagons and ambulances moved lazily about laden with rations and the wounded. Arms were stacked and troops were resting and waiting with passing indifference the coming storm, maybe dreaming of home, forgetful of surrounding horrors and coming dangers. Surgeons and nurses were busy with the wounded, who had taken temporary shelter in barns with the animals. Couriers were speeding to and from General Meade's headquarters. The old German sat on the doorstep in meditative silence, smoking some Virginia weed just imported. Katrina was looking after the children secreted in the loft. With us expectation was so intense that we were afraid to speak, lest the sound of the human voice would precipitate the avalanche we wished for, yet dreaded.

Suddenly without threat or warning, like a clap of thunder in a clear sky, a storm of shot, shrieking shell and the roar of two hundred cannon seemed to fill all space above the trembling earth. Horses galloped riderless over the field or sank down bleeding and beating the earth with broken limbs. The barns were on fire, a hundred thousand men sprang from the ground,

Sarah and Jacob Weikert's stone house on the eastern slope of Little Round Top. This large farm became a field hospital for the Union Fifth Corps and held the shattered bodies of many of Colonel Powell's veterans.

called to action by a blast more potent than Roderick's horn.

A Comic Interlude.

The old German promptly took refuge in the well, and "we knew by the smoke which so gracefully curled" that his pipe was the companion of his fear. The old wife left her chickens to look after Fritz. The treacherous smoke betrayed his hiding place. We thought she intended to join him in his retreat when she made a rush for the well, but to our surprise she seemed unconcious of danger from the flying missiles which fell around her, but danced around the well, frantically imploring him to come out. She said he would "die mit cold." He only replied, "Mine Cot, Katrine! Nein, nein!"

The conflict raged and the incessant roar and augmenting thunders of artillery supplying the chorusus to rattling musketry expressed the supreme grandeur of battle. We did not see the conquering Confederates coming. The trained ear of the soldier enables him to mark the progress of battle. We felt each movement and hope rose high as Pickett's men, like the rush of many waters, lashed with storming fury the enemy's solid and bristling front. Then despair expelled hope when they receded, broken and bleeding. We were grief-stricken, sick at heart and wearied with the tumultuous emotions of the battle's storm.

What The Eye Saw.

I observed much which escaped the eyes of the active participants. The line of battle was a crescent, the inner shorter line occupied by the Union forces and was more elevated than the Confederate batteries. Their front was both the post of honor and place of better protection than could be found in the rear. A retreat from their defenses exposed them to the deliberate fire of the charging infantry; the shell and shot from the Confederate batteries, passing over their heads when close to their works, plunged to the earth immediately in their rear and swept with concentrated violence every part of the encircled space. If such a condition had have been needed, here was an instance of obliged valor and sturdy tenacity. The opening cannonade drove all the waiting troops in the rear to the protection offered near the front. Thus the reserves were at hand and could file into their places at a moment's notice without exposure. [19]

The surgeons and nurses about the burning barns hastily left their post and fled in dismay. The plaints of burning beasts and the cries of the wounded added to these opening horrors. The slightly wounded of both parties responded to this call of humanity and nobly labored to save the helpless. Many were stricken down while bearing a comrade or a foe to a safe retreat, which could only be found in a ditch or sheltering rock. Wrecked ambulances, wagons and dead horses afforded precarious protection to some who could not find anything better. [20]

A Gallant Rider.

A dashing young officer, riding a splendid black horse, came flying across the field towards us. We watched him with interest and anxiety. Foe though he was, we wished him a safe deliverance from his battle-scraped space. On he came and had almost passed the line of danger. We gave him a cheer and just as he raised his hand to acknowledge our token horse and rider went down in death almost at the feet of the old woman who still hung over the curb of the well. Hundreds of conflagrations occurred during the day and at night the smouldering fires gleamed like gory beacons scattered over the gloomy waste. The tramp and hum of moving men retiring to the rear seeking rest and such refreshments as could be obtained awoke our interest in the results of the day.

We heard wonderful tales of the battle and learned that our people were beaten and our worst fears confirmed. This was a gloomy night [July 3] and we wished we were lying in the valley with our dead. As prisoners, we were lost to our country; as men we were enduring the tortures which restraint entails and mortification inflicts.

Among Wounded Prisoners.

The morning dawned upon a different spectacle than that which had graced the hills and valleys two days before. The pomp was gone and the grandeur faded. During the night the dead had been drawn to the rear and laid in long regular lines by the rude undertakers of the army. They were mustered for the last time and the ghastly parade was ready to march to the tomb.

In a few hours it became evident that the battle of Gettysburg had been fought and won and the leading incidents had passed into history.

Surgeons and attendants were distressingly slow in making their appearance. Provisions and hospital stores were scarce. Water! water! was the cry of hundreds and many resorted to the crimson pools wherever they could be found. Field officers, followed by couriers, like an army with little banners, were busily moving around in every direction occupied with their especial duties. Thus passed the first day after the battle.[21]

Visitors To The Field.

The night was more dreary, the troops were gone and wounded and dead were the sole possessors of the field of glory. Many died during this interval who might have been saved. I knew one man who slew himself rather than endure further torture and suffering.[22]

The third day of volunteer aid came to the rescue. Tents were erected, men and women joined the infirmary corps in the noble work of supplying the wants and ministering to the needs of the wounded. After these workers came the Christian and political missionaries and a vast concourse of sightseers, whole families with the baby.

The Sight-Seers.

The big show was gone, but they seemed content to look over the ground where it had been. A torn and bloody garment would attract a crowd, which would disperse only to concentrate again to look at a hat perforated by bullets. Moving from that to a dismantled gun carriage, chief among the objects of interest was a field piece with the muzzle plugged by a Confederate shot.[23] The habiliments of the men and variegated plumage of the women made an interesting scene. The typical farmer, the German costumed in clothes of the last century, the village belle and the country housewife, all moving in pursuit of the same object and animated only by idle curiosity, seeming without thought or care for the hundreds of suffering men lying so near them without notice or sympathy.[24]

Idle Curiosity.

This suggested the idea that deeds of daring, while claiming the admiration of the world, do not always cause interest among men for the actors themselves. This vast concourse visiting the scene of achievements of which they were proud seemed to have no interest in the individuals themselves.

It was not until the evening of the third day after the battle [July 6] that we received any attention except from the mentioned members of the Fourteenth United States Regulars. They were about us, whether as guards or companions, we did not know. We were taken that night to a tent and lost sight of them.[25]

Distinguished Visitors.

There were eighteen of us in an open tent. Just outside and under what

Governor Andrew Curtin of Pennsylvania visited the field hospital where Colonel Powell and other wounded rebels lay.

Michael Fiscel's farm where Robert Powell may have been visited by the governor of Pennsylvania.

is called an individual tent was self-quartered a peculiar specimen known as wild Texan, who occupied himself looking after and nursing fourteen wounds. Among our first visitors was the Governor of Pennsylvania, who looked as if he had been roughing it with his militia.[26] His companions were new and fresh all over, painfullly and embarrassing new. One of the party approached the human fragments under the little strip of canvas and asked: "What can I do for you, my good fellow?" "Well, mister," he replied, "now you don't think I am good and I am not a feller. We uns didn't come among you uns to ask favors, and I reckon I will just remember the fourteen I got and not be obligating myself to you for anything better." That man finally escaped and reached the "Land of Dixie."

A Good Angel In Black.

The visit of "the mysterious lady," as we called her, was an event altogether pleasant; but while it threw a radiance over the gloom which darkened around us it was connected with an event common among us. She was dressed in deep mourning and was standing in our presence before we were aware of her approach. She was earnestly, almost eagerly, surveying the dirty wretches before her. We were so unpresentable that we were ashamed and forgot our manners and failed to make courteous recognition of her kindly visit. We knew the visit was one of kindness, for women do not often get so near suffering without an intention of doing good.

Death Of A Youth.

In our tent was a boy-soldier, so remarkable for his comeliness and just then he was almost beautiful; the fever had subsided and all suffering past; he was experiencing that deluding feeling of absolute rest and repose which precedes dissolution. He was patiently awaiting the final summons, made inevitable because the surgeon's knife had not yet made its bloody rounds. Noticing a lady visitor, his eyes brightened and gazing at her a moment with a look of affectionate longing, he said:
"Excuse me, lady, but oh, you remind me so much of my mother."
She immediately placed herself on the ground beside him and put his head in her lap and smoothed and caressed him until life was extinct. With prompt preparation she went away, taking his body with her.

A Humorous Episode.

The next day there was unusual commotion among the inhabitants of this village of tents. Surgeons, nurses and cooks gathered in groups, talking and making significant gestures and pointing to a tent occupied by the prisoners. They walked by and looked in as if the tent contained something of great interest. The excitement and extraordinary behavior created concern and uneasiness among the prisoners, who wondered what new calamity had befallen them. The surprise culminated and the mysterious movements partially solved, when an ambulance containing two Union officers, escorted by a squad of cavalry, dashed up to the tent, from which was taken a Con-

23

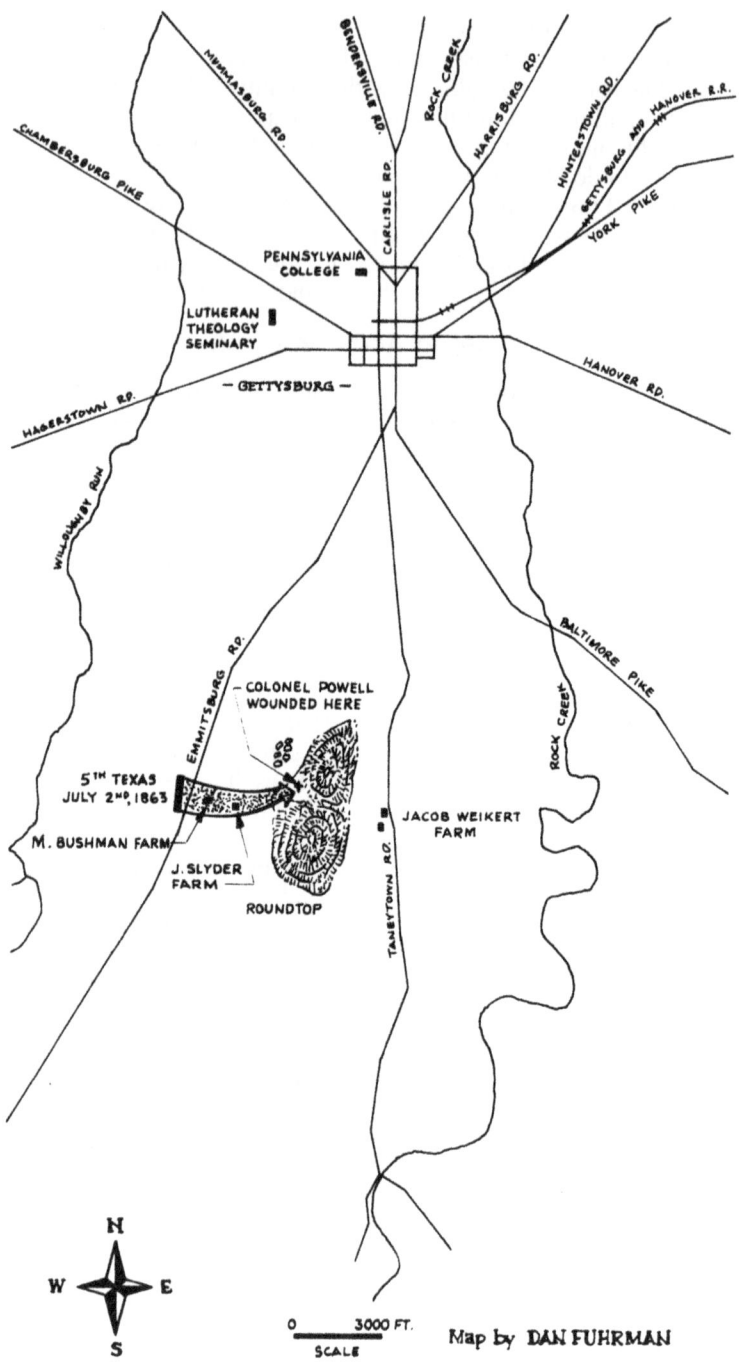

PENNSYLVANIA
COLLEGE

LUTHERAN
THEOLOGY
SEMINARY

— GETTYSBURG —

CHAMBERSBURG PIKE

MUMMASBURG RD.

BENDERSVILLE RD.

CARLISLE RD.

ROCK CREEK

HARRISBURG RD.

HUNTERSTOWN RD.

GETTYSBURG AND HANOVER R.R.

YORK PIKE

HANOVER RD.

HAGERSTOWN RD.

WILLOUGHBY RUN

EMMITSBURG RD.

— COLONEL POWELL
WOUNDED HERE

5TH TEXAS
JULY 2ND, 1863

M. BUSHMAN FARM

J. SLYDER
FARM

ROUNDTOP

BALTIMORE PIKE

ROCK CREEK

JACOB WEIKERT
FARM

TANEYTOWN RD.

N
W   E
S

0   3000 FT.
        SCALE

Map by DAN FUHRMAN

24

This bronze tablet on Warfield Ridge indicates where the 5th Texas Infantry and Robertson's brigade deployed prior to their attack eastward toward Little Round Top.

The iron marker on the crest of Houck's Ridge is near where a portion of Robertson's brigade first struck the Union battle line on July 2. The 5th Texas was engaged several hundred yards to the left or east of this spot.

federate officer in the uniform of a colonel. Entering the ambulance with him they were driven rapidly toward Gettysburg, much to the discomfort of the wounded officer, who protested in vain and inquired without getting any satisfaction as to these summary proceedings. On reaching the headquarters of the Provost Marshal he was subjected to a rigid examination, and informed that it was useless to attempt to disguise himself any longer, as he was fully identified as General Longstreet.[27]

A Mare's Nest.

There was much hilarity and congratulations among the party who had made this important discovery. They seemed to think thay had one of the pillars of the Confederacy and now the edifice must fall. He was confined in a room in the college building,[28] which were then occupied entirely by Confederate prisoners, who were greatly excited when the news spread among them that General Longstreet had been captured and was now a prisoner in the house. Some of his friends hurried to see him and when they reported the result of their observations, captive rebeldom smiled and the smile widened into a broad grin.

The College Edifice where Colonel Powell and almost 900 other Confederate wounded recuperated for several weeks after the battle.

The Guardsmen.

Two youthful militiamen fresh from the harvest fields and "truck patches" stood guard at the door with instructions not to lose sight of their prisoner a moment. The door was open and their guns were crossed before it. They tried to while away the time by singing and whistling alternate lines of "When This Cruel War is Over" until their prisoner was nearly distracted. He had a little conversation with them, but they were not certain that their duties as guards would permit such rational diversion. They ventured, however, to express their opinion of government hard-tack and spoke with fond recollections of their home-made bread, explained that their mothers baked once a week, every Thursday, and when it was two days' old it was "sad" bread and was then in its prime.

On Exhibiton.

The news having gone abroad that Longstreet was a prisoner made this doubly-guarded room the centre of interest, and a procession of townspeople filed through the passage to see the great soldier. Occasionally a Confederate would flit by whose face told too plainly how he was enjoying the huge joke. Some officers, brilliant with tinsel and new clothes, entered without ceremony to make a close inspection of this human wonder, a rebel lieutenant general. They discussed him as if he was not a sentient being, spoke of him, not to him, and freely expressed their opinion that he was bound to pull hemp, as all the Confederate chiefs must do sooner or later. The officer felt happy in the knowledge that the man who had so stoutly and faithfully sustained our cause was not just then in danger of the hangman's rope, and had gone with the Confederate army to contest other fields.

The president of the college[29] presented himself to interview General Lee's favorite lieutenant, leading, or rather dragging, a ten-year-old boy, whose eyes, as he peeps from behind his father's coat tail, blazing with eager curiosity, were framed in a face expressing the agony of fear. The president was a man of fine presence, engaging manners and conversation made impressive by a benign countenance. After a few words of patronizing salutation he made a little speech.

"The Terrible Rebel."

The officer protested that he was mistaken in his identity and that he knew nothing of General Lee's plans (as the professor had intimated), but was satisfied that neither the Confederate armies nor people were dismayed or demoralized and would continue the conflict to the bitter end, regardless of consequences. While this conversation was in progress the little boy, having thoroughly prospected the small apartment, timidly approached the terrible Confederate, looked him over, looked around him and under him and then resting his head upon his knee gazed in his face a moment with confidence and then turned an inquiring look to his father, intimating that his little head had conceived the idea that the twig had been bent out of the perpendicular.

27

Pennsylvania College president Henry Lewis Baugher.

Colonel Powell may have incorrectly believed that Professor Michael Jacobs was the president of Pennsylvania College.

Making Friends.

The officer, taking the willing hand of the little fellow, told him that he had left a son at home about his age, with eyes and hair just the color of his, who loved his father and did not think he was a bad man. On leaving he said to his father that he did not see that rebels were different from other people. That was nearly twenty-one years ago. The boys are men now. How are the two inclined? The president did not omit a doxology to the "old flag, the flag of our fathers," as he left.

A Masked Gun.

Immediately after the departure of these interesting guests there appeared at the door a person dressed in the uniform of a Confederate surgeon, closely guarded, and after some seeming difficulty succeeded in gaining admission. He appeared to be laboring under some excitement and was distrait and uncomfortable. After some hesitation he said: "General, I hope you recognize me as Assistant Surgeon_____, of the _____Mississippi Regiment." I was assistant surgeon of Dr. Groves,[30] who died in this room. He further explained that when all of the surgeons whom General Lee had left in charge of his own and the enemy's wounded who had fallen in his hands were arrested he was absent from his quarters soliciting supplies from the neighboring farmers, and I am now under arrest as a spy.

The Mouse Smelt Out.

The supposed Longstreet knew the surgeons had been made prisoners and that Dr. Groves died in that room—for his body was removed after he entered it—but could not understand how it was that any medical officer in the Army of Northern Virginia could be ignorant of the personal appearance of General Longstreet. Here was a mystery under which lay hope or danger. The situation was exciting. A prisoner is all expectation, impatient for something to turn up and ready for any enterprise, however hazardous, if there is a hope of liberty at the end. At the beginning of this interview there was manifest anxiety or curiosity among the lady visitors and nurses. They crowded about the door and of course the officer's eyes were there and perhaps his heart, too.

Queer Maneuvers.

He soon understood that he must be communicated with before giving any confidence to his visitor. At last a book appeared. It was presented with a fringe inserted between the leaves and received in the same way. Opening it the word "spy" was prominent. Thus warned he was prepared to deal with the vile wretch who had come to seek confidence to betray it. After this interruption the "spy" drew nearer, so as not to be overheard, and said in a whisper "that if it could be satisfactorily established that he was a Confederate surgeon he would be released on parole and have the liberty of the buildings and grounds occupied by our own people, and would be able, with outside help, to disarm the guard, take their guns and all who

29

were able to move could make their escape."[31]

The "Spy" Rebuked.

It was a delicate task to get rid of this dangerous person without exciting a suspicion that he was detected and his character and wicked purposes understood, which was to create a pretext for the wholesale slaughter of the prisoners and implicate the ladies who were volunteer nurses and sympathizers as accessories, aiders and abettors in the plan outlined by himself. The officer told him that he could not recognize him; that it was impossible for him to know all the surgeons and assistant surgeons in the army; that he had acted indiscreetly in leaving his post and roaming over the country as forager to a hospital; besides, the surgeons had just left for Baltimore and would probably be detained there long enough for him to get their evidence as to his position; that the Federal Government was not so anxious to shed a few drops of blood and take the life of one little man as to hang him up without giving him a fair chance to defend himself. The spy took his departure, seemingly despondent and disappointed.

A few days after we were rejoiced to hear that General Lee had overcome the defiant waters of the Potomac and trod once more his native heath. Longstreet was heard from and his counterfeit subsided to the level of other prisoners and was permitted to draw his rations, emerge from solitude and receive his friends.

As I have said, the college building was a temporary hospital, occupied mostly by wounded Confederates. The Confederate surgeons were confined here, also, after their arrest and it was the centre of attraction to all visitors. These were mostly ladies and Confederate sympathizers. Dr. Shivers,[32] the surgeon in charge, was supremely disgusted that he was not the centre figure in this tableau and swore by Mars that the show should close. In this hospital was suffering and death and yet there was room and opportunity for fun, frolic and intrigue. Cupid held his court in defiance of guards and even death seemed to hold back his darts and give triumph to love.

Going to School.

A Miss E.,[33] supposing disloyalty the result of ignorance, undertook to open a branch of the public school. "Uncle Sam" footing the bills for house rent, board for pupils, janitors and servants, the teacher giving her service gratis. She procured primers, organized classes among the men and formally opened school. Professors and jurists, with books spread on upturned coffee-pots, primitive thumb papers and pointers in hand, gravely and seriously attacked the mysteries of the alphabet. They whined in infantile treble A B C with the stupid hesitancy and amazed reluctance of a four-year-old juvenile.

From Bad to Worse.

But these were days of swift events and every hour we were confronted

The east side of the Lutheran Theological Seminary's main building. It became a hospital and prison for Powell and other rebel officers.

with something new, all going from bad to worse. We were surrendered to the keeping of the militia, the last old soldier was gone and with him all our little liberties and our sense of security. An old soldier, when guarding prisoners, deports himself after the manner of the lion watching the gambols of their young, restraining and protecting them. They who meet strong and brave men with arms in their hands are not afraid of them, nor do they persecute them when they are unarmed.

At The Seminary.

About this time I was transferred to the Seminary,[34] where there were only a few Confederate officers, the buildings being almost exclusively appropriated to the use of wounded Federal officers. Here, also, we found the militia acting in the capacity of servants to their wounded officers, but saving their character as soldiers by guarding Generals Trimble and Kemper and Major Douglass and myself. General Trimble was minus a leg; General Kemper was considered fatally wounded.[35] Two guards were posted at each door of the three rooms and the utmost vigilance enjoined and all the formalities observed in mounting and relieving guard.

With Major Douglass.[36]

Douglass and I were the only prisoners able to leave their cots. Yet when

31

Major General Isaac Ridgeway Trimble, minus a leg lost on July 3, became an unwilling patient at Gettysburg's Lutheran Theological Seminary.

Brigadier General James Lawson Kemper, wounded and captured on the last day of the battle, spent many hours in the Seminary Hospital flirting with visiting women and tormenting his Yankee captors.

a door opened the guards promptly came to the "make ready." Douglass had been "Stonewall" Jackson's aid. I was a Texan and credited with dining on negroes and unhappy unless I killed a man every morning before breakfast.

I was rooming with Major Douglass and one day we were visited by some ladies prospecting for Confederates. We were not the least alarmed; indeed, the presence and sight of women was refreshing. The Major was charming and always successful in his efforts to entertain when ladies constituted the audience. When they left, a pretty young lady lingered behind and surreptitiously handed him a red apple. As she reached the door she hesitated a moment and threw one to me. "Victory, victory!" was the cry when the door closed as we held aloft our much-prized fruit.

One day, while walking the long hall accompanied by one of the militia as guard and escort with his gun held in the position of "make ready," we met a handsome lady, who seemed to command marked respect, and I inquired as to whom she was. The guard replied that she was the "colonel's woman," pointing to a room occupied by a wounded officer. It was the first time I ever heard a wife so designated.

The youthful Major Henry Kyd Douglas, also a "roommate" of Colonel Powell's, had been seriously wounded in the left shoulder at Culp's Hill on July 3.

Annoying Amateur Guards.

The rules regulating the conduct of the prisoners grew more stringent every day. A prisoner or a visitor conforming to and observant of the regulations of yesterday was surprised and disciplined for violating the regulations of today. The four prisoners kept a militia company in a state of feverish agitation and anxiety. I was permitted one day to go into the room occupied by General Kemper. Some ladies of intensely loyal inclinations were making him a visit. They rehearsed the little speech and with some ornate rhetoric made manifest their hostility to all Confederates and their cause. Now Kemper was a man of warm and quick temper, but of gracious speech and courtly manners. I was advised by a wicked glance of his eye that he intended to make a conquest of these zealous dames.

Kemper's Conquest.

His conversation was sparkling and brilliant. Woman, not war, was his theme. We forgot for the time that there was war and were in a land peopled by fairies, whose sole occupation was to minister to the afflicted. The ladies, forgetting their mission, personated his fairies, moved their seats nearer and, while one used her grateful fan to cool his fevered brow, the other bathed his parched and burning hands. His eyes sparkled with triumph as he quoted with feeling effect the lines of Scott, "Oh, woman, in our hours of ease." After this flash and excited effort he relapsed into a state of painful weariness. Handkerchiefs were in requisition to stay the evidences of sympathy. His visitors bid him a reluctant good-bye and, perhaps for the first time, comprehended the words of our Lord, "Love your enemies."

An Odd Proceeding.

Two other ladies, who were friends and sympathizers, entered his room by special permission and while yet in the room the same authority who granted the permission to make the visit became alarmed and issued orders forbidding any lady to pass in or out of his door. So when they had completed their visit and approached the door on their way out they were halted and informed that they could not pass, as orders were issued to hold them prisoners in that room. Now there were more tears and more handkerchiefs. An officer and a Confederate prisoner who was present attempted to remonstrate with the guard at the door. He was repelled in language too vile to repeat. Kemper called from his cot: "Kill them! kill them!" The officer exhibited his penknife as if in compliance of his request.

The guard fled down the long hall, the ladies passed out, the officer giving his knife to one of them. A militia captain with a squad of men soon made his appearance, had the offender searched for concealed weapons, and under guard of a whole company was marched through the town with pomp and circumstance to the railroad depot and incarcerated in a box car filled with the bodies of dead men, the whole reeking and black with ichor.

A Friend In Need.

A Federal soldier, though a boy, felt akin to this hapless Confederate officer and his heart glowed with gratitude for a service which, he declared, his command had done him in the second battle of Manassas. His name was Jack Howard. He followed the prisoner, took in the situation and acted the part of a good Samaritan by supplying him with whisky, a pipe and tobacco, at the same time expressing his gratification at being able to return a favor. Jack was an Irish lad and when interrogated how he had been benefitted or served by this officer's Confederate command gave the following Irish explanation. He said he met Hood's Texans at Manassas, he then belonging to the red breeches zouaves. "Ye see," he added, "thim Texans kilt all av us but foorteen an' we wur retired to the infirmary corps to remane in the rear an' attind the wounded in field hospitals." He said he had only one relative in America and that relative was a Confederate soldier in the Fifth Texas Regiment.[37]

The view through a window of the Seminary building where Colonel Powell lived for several weeks after being wounded at Gettysburg.

EPILOGUE

After spending several weeks in the field hospital at the Lutheran Theological Seminary, Colonel Powell was sent to Johnson's Island in Ohio and confined in the Federal prison camp there until January 1865. Late in that month he was transferred to Fort Monroe where he was paroled on February 6, 1865, two months before the war ended. Powell immediately took command of Hood's old Texas Brigade and was present with his command throughout the final months of the siege of Petersburg and later Lee's retreat westward from April 2 to the 9th when the Army of Northern Virginia was surrendered at Appomattox Court House in Virginia. Colonel Powell himself was paroled on April 12, along with 12 officers and 149 enlisted men of the 5th Texas, a fairly large regiment at that surrender.

Robert Powell returned to Texas where he lived for eighteen years. In 1882 he moved to St. Louis, Missouri, where he resided for a time at 4314 Maryland Avenue. His reminiscense of Gettysburg may have been written during this early period in that city.[1]

Although Powell lived almost 700 miles from his old Texas home, he remained very active in reunions and veterans' affairs. For instance, during the 1889 reunion of Hood's Texas Brigade which was held in Waco, Texas, it was reported that Colonel Powell had attended, bringing with him from St. Louis one of the original battle flags of the Fifth Texas. The tattered and torn and honored emblem "hung over the main window of the platform," where one veteran of the 5th said as he gazed upon it that, "smoke appeared to ascend from the faded and ragged banner, and the sound of musketry and cannon came faintly like a dream of an echo heard in a tomb."[2]

Colonel Robert M. Powell lived a full and interesting life until his death at age 90. He died of pneumonia in St. Louis on January 15, 1916.

APPENDIX I

Report of Lieut. Col. K. Bryan, Fifth Texas Infantry.
Near Hagerstown, MD., July 8, 1863.

SIR: Col. R. M. Powell having fallen into the hands of the enemy, it devolves upon me, as lieutenant-colonel of the regiment, to report the part taken by it as far as came under my observation in the action of July 2 and 3, near Gettysburg, Pa.

About 4 p.m. on the 2d instant, General Hood's division was drawn up in line of battle fronting the heights occupied by the enemy. The Fifth Texas Regiment occupied the right of the brigade, resting on General Law's left, whose brigade was the one of direction. At the word "Forward," the regiment moved forward in good order. The enemy had a line of sharp-shooters at the foot of the first height, behind a stone fence, about three-fourths of a mile from our starting point, which distance was passed over by our line at a double-quick and a run.

At our approach, the enemy retired to the top of the first height, protected by a ledge of rocks. A short halt was made at the stone fence, to enable those who had fallen behind to regain their places. When the command "Forward" again fell from the lips of our gallant colonel, every man leaped the fence, and advanced rapidly up the hillside. The enemy again fled at our approach, sheltering himself behind his fortified position on the top of the second height, about 200 yards distant from the first.

From this position we failed to drive them. Our failure was owing to the rocky nature of the ground over which we had to pass, the huge rocks forming defiles through which not more than 3 or 4 men could pass abreast, thus breaking up our alignment and rendering its reformation impossible. Notwithstanding the difficulties to overcome, the men pressed on to the pass of the precipitous stronghold, forming and securing the enemy's second position, many of our officers and men falling in passing the open space between the heights. Here we halted, there being small clusters of rocks far below the elevated position of the enemy, which gave us partial protection. From this position we were enabled to deliver our fire for the first time with accuracy.

Seeing that the men were in the best obtainable position, and deeming a farther advance without re-enforcements impracticable (a great many of the regiment having been already disabled), I looked for Colonel Powell, to know his next order. Failing to see him, I concluded at once that he, like many of his gallant officers and men, had fallen a victim to the deadly missiles of the enemy, which were being showered like hail upon us. I moved toward the center, passing many officers and men who had fallen, having discharged their whole duty like true soldiers. I had not proceeded far when I discovered the prostrate form of our noble colonel, who had fallen at his post, his face to the foe. I hastened toward him, when I received a wound in my left arm. On reaching the colonel, I found that he was not dead; but seeing the rent in his coat where the ball had passed out, my fears were excited that his wound would prove mortal. The hemorrhage from my own wound forced me from the field, leaving the command upon Major Rogers.

The officers and men of my wing of the regiment continued to discharge their duties in a manner worthy of our cause so long as I remained upon the field, and from their conduct heretofore I would not hesitate to vouch for them during the remainder of the battle.

Captain [John S.] Cleveland, of Company H, was on the right. His skillful management of his own company aided me vastly in the direction of my wing.

K. BRYAN
Lieutenant-Colonel Fifth Texas Regiment.
Lieut. JOHN W. KERR, Acting Assistant Adjutant-General.

Report of Maj. J.C. Rogers, Fifth Texas Infantry.
NEAR HAGERSTOWN, MD.,
July 8, 1863.

SIR: I have the honor to forward a continuation of the report of the part taken by the Fifth Texas Regiment in the action of the 2d and 3d instant, after the wounding of Colonels Powell and Bryan, when the command devolved upon me, the regiment still holding the position as left by Colonel Bryan, firing with accuracy and deadly effect.

The order to fall back came from some unknown source, and, finding that the regiments on our right and left had retired, it became necessary to follow. I therefore gave the order for the regiment to about-face and retire to the rear, which they did in good order until they reached the position mentioned in Colonel Bryan's report as the second position of the enemy, and here were halted and reformed, in connection with the other regiments. From the exhausted condition of the men, it was deemed necessary to remain here for a few moments.

The regiments were again ordered forward, which they did in the most gallant manner, and regained their first position, which they held as long as it was tenable; and a farther advance being impracticable, owing to the nature of the ground, as expressed in Colonel Bryan's report, they again retired in good order to an open space about 50 yards in rear, when here it was discovered for the first time that nearly two-thirds of our officers and men had been killed and wounded.

Only a few moments were here consumed to allow the men to recover their breath, when, in obedience to orders, I again moved the regiment forward to attack the enemy in their impregnable fortification. We held this position until it was discovered that we had no supports either on the right or left, and were about to be flanked, and therefore were again compelled to retire, which the regiment did in good order to the point mentioned in Colonel Bryan's report as the second position of the enemy, which place we were ordered to hold at all hazards, which we did.

Just before day on the morning of the 3d, orders reached me that breastworks must be thrown up, and the position held. The order was obeyed. During the day, constant skirmishing was kept up with the enemy, which resulted in the loss to us of many of our best scouts. Late in the evening, in obedience to orders, I about-faced my regiment, and marched three-quarters of a mile to the crest of the ridge from which the charge of the day previous commenced. Here we threw up breastworks, behind which we remained during the night.

I would respectfully beg leave to call attention to the valuable assistance I received from Capt. John S. Cleveland in the management of the right wing of my regiment, and Capt. T. T. Clay on the left; also, to the heroic conduct of T. W. Fitzgerald, of Company A, who was color-bearer. He pressed gallantly forward, and was badly wounded far in front. J. A. Howard, of Company B, color corporal, then took the flag, and remained firmly at his post. He was almost instantly killed. The colors were then taken by Sergt. W. Evans, of Company F, who planted them defiantly in the face of the foe during the remainder of the fight, always advancing promptly to the front when the order was given.

The general conduct of officers and men was beyond all praise.

J. C. ROGERS,
Major, Commanding Fifth Texas Regiment.

Lieut. JOHN W. KERR,
Acting Assistant Adjutant-General.

APPENDIX II

Soldiers of the 5th Texas killed or mortally wounded with Colonel R.M. Powell in the attack on Little Round Top, July 2, 1863.

NAME	COMPANY	BURIAL SITE
W.P. Anderson	G	
Thomas Bates	I	
Albert Baudwin	F	
M.W. Blackman	G	
John Boothe	E	U.S. Fifth Corps, 2nd Division hospital at Jane Clapsaddle's farm on Lousy Run
Charles D. Brashear	F	
Sgt. James T. Carter	B	
S. Cohen	A	
Cpl. George W. Counts	E	
C.W. Deggs	A	J. Edward Plank farm under tree to the front and right of house
Sgt. Z.Y. Dezell	C	
N. Douglas	D	
Sim Dunn	K	
G.W. Eskridge	D	
W.H.H. Fields	K	
Frank M. Fitzgerald	H	
Lt. C.A. Graham	I	
William Haley	I	
Henry Haynes	B	
Lt. D.H. Henderson	B	
James L. Holmes	I	J. Edward Plank farm under tree to the front and right of house
Cpl. J.A. Howard	B	
Richard S. Hudson	E	
M. Hurley	B	
Andrew Jackson	G	Under apple tree near road at U.S. Third Corps hospital
Cpl. John A. Jolly	G	
G.A. Jones	G	
W.C. Jones	G	
S.S. Lockett	E	Michael Fiscel's farm on east side of woods
J.D. Locklin	G	
Joseph E. Love	A	
J.A. McDade	D	
William McDowell	A	

T.C. Matthews	K	
J.P. Meece	K	J. Edward Plank farm under tree to the front and right of house
Cpl. John S. Miller	B	
William F. Nelms	B	At 2nd Division, U.S. Fifth Corps hospital, south of Jane Clapsaddle's farmhouse
John O'Neill	B	
James H. Poole	C	
Henry Pratt	B	
Marshal Prue	F	Near the base of Round Top in a field between Rock Creek and the Turnpike below the rocks in the lower part of a meadow
William Sensebaugh	E	At Jesse Worley's farm west of Two Taverns
A.G. Sloan	B	
John Smith	B	
William E. Stevens	E	Burial yard, U.S. General Hospital, Row 6 or 7, Grave 11, died September 4, 1863
S.V. Stevenson	H	
William Turner	D	
Sgt. J.J. Walthall	E	J. Edward Plank farm under tree to the front and right of house
Sam H. Watson	E	Burial yard, U.S. General Hospital, Row 8, Grave 3, died September 10, 1863
Thomas Weatherby	E	
J.R. Weathers	H	
J.W. Webb	G	
Peter G. Williamson	D	Burial yard, U.S. General Hospital, Row 6 or 7, Grave 15, died September 6, 1863
W.B. Wilson	B	

NOTES TO INTRODUCTION

1. The Philadelphia *Weekly Times* for a time between 1877 and 1888, ran a series of Civil War articles under the title "Annals of the War." The editor was A.K. McClure. Many well known officers sent in articles to be published, including Powell's chief, General James Longstreet. Powell's subtitle on this particular article stated: "The Experiences of a Texas Officer in one of the Charges at Little Round Top."

2. Montgomery County, Texas is the area just north of Harris County. Harris includes the city of Houston, barely within its boundaries. Danville is no longer listed on a modern-day map of Texas. I lived for several years just northwest of this county and spent a great deal of time on Walnut Creek Ranch which was in Montgomery County. The back roads, creeks and small towns became very familiar to me, and I remember well the places where many of the men of the 5th Texas regiment hailed from. Nearby in Bryan stood an old brick building where men of what would become Hood's Brigade met in the early days of the war to form their units. Hood's Texas Brigade contained approximately 5,300 men during the war including some men from Arkansas. 617 veterans of this organization surrendered at Appomattox.

3. Harrisburg, Texas is now Houston, named for Samuel Houston who was born in Virginia in 1793. In 1861 he had been governor of Texas for almost two years, and was opposed to secession, favoring Texas independence over uniting with other Southern states if the Union was dissolved. Houston refused to take the oath of loyalty to the Confederacy in March of 1861, resigned the governorship and retired to his house in Huntsville, Texas. He died in July of 1863.

4. Joseph H. Crute, Jr. *Units of the Confederate States Army.* Derwent Books, Midlothian, Virginia, 1987, p. 326. The 5th was recruited in the counties of Harris, Colorado, Leon, Walker, Montgomery, Washington, Jefferson, Liberty, Milam, Polk, and Trinity. Jefferson Davis authorized the forming of the *brigade* in Richmond in October, 1861.

5. W.J. Tancig. *Confederate Military Land Units, 1861-1865.* Thomas Yoseloff, New York, 1967, p. 89. Early in the war most companies picked a nickname to identify their local and individual units. These names soon fell by the wayside as the men took on the identities of the new regiments.

6. W.A. Nabours, "Active Service of a Texas Command," *Confederate Veteran* Magazine, #24, 1916, p. 69. In the months following Gettysburg, the 5th Texas was sent with Longstreet's Corps to reinforce General Braxton Bragg's army in Tennessee. The regiment took part in the siege of Knoxville, and other actions in the eastern part of that state. Later the corps returned to Virginia where they went through part of the Wilderness engagement, Spotsylvania, and Cold Harbor. Next the 5th was moved to the James River, below Richmond, then to Petersburg where they remained for a time. Once again to the north side of the James where they were in the defense of the Fort Gilmore — New Market Heights — Deep Bottom areas. With the evacuation of Richmond and Petersburg in the spring of 1865, the 5th formed part of Lee's rear guard during the retreat to Appomattox. The unit had then been in service three years, eight months and about nine days. After the surrender each man

was on his own with no food, no extra clothes and no money, on a trek which took them over a thousand miles toward home through a mostly devastated country.

7. At this battle the 5th Texas lost fifteen killed and 224 wounded, one of the highest casualty figures in the engagement. At Gaines' Mill they suffered greatly in several daring charges, and were in the forefront of the fighting at Antietam where two-thirds of the brigade fell in action.

William F. Fox. *Regimental Losses in the American Civil War.* A.S. Brandow Printing, Albany, New York, 1898.

8. Robert K. Krick. *Lee's Colonels.* 2nd edition, Press of Morningside Bookshop, Dayton, Ohio, 1984, p. 265.

9. Robert K. Krick. *The Gettysburg Death Roster.* Press of Morningside Bookshop, Dayton, Ohio, 1981, p. 8.

Joseph H. Crute, Jr., op cit., p. 326.

At Gettysburg Powell's lieutenant colonel was King Bryan; his major was Jefferson C. Rogers. See Appendix I for their reports of the battle after Powell was wounded.

The company commanders were:

A — Captain D.C. Farmer (wounded)
B — Captain J.D. Roberdeau (captured)
C — Captain J.J. McBride
D — Captain W.T. Hill (wounded)
E — Captain T.A. Baber
F — Captain W.D. Williams (wounded)
G — Captain John Smith
H — Captain J.S. Cleveland
I — Captain T.T. Clay
K — Captain R.W. Hubert (captured)

Captain T.T. Clay, Company I, 5th Texas was near Powell in the disastrous attack on Little Round Top.

43

NOTES TO "RECOLLECTIONS"

1. Powell actually began his original narrative while his brigade was near Suffolk, Virginia. The first several paragraphs dealt with General James Longstreets' Corps' activities foraging in that area, and holding enemy forces at bay with some skirmishing and sharpshooting. Their adversaries here were part of the Union Ninth Corps under General George W. Getty. For more on this situation see Mark M. Boatner, *The Civil War Dictionary*, p. 817.

On May 2, 1863, Powell says Longstreet's Corps was recalled to the Richmond area to join General Robert E. Lee's army which was preparing to move northward, a move which really did not begin until the first week of June.

2. One of the standard comments by Confederate soldiers who campaigned in Maryland and Pennsylvania was their awe at the wealth and prosperity of these Northern people. This fact alone must have discouraged thousands of even Lee's most resolute veterans. Many could not see how the war could be won against a foe so rich, and a land and population seemingly so unaffected by war. For instance, one captured rebel soldier told Private Reuben Ruch of the 153rd Pennsylvania Infantry that, "...there was no use fighting the North for he had never seen such a rich country as Pennsylvania and that [the] towns were yet full of men, in fact a fellow would not miss those that were in the army."

Another Confederate, John C. West of the 4th Texas Infantry said of Pennsylvania and Maryland:

> The portions of the two last mentioned states through which we passed are the most thoroughly improved which I ever saw. There was not a foot of surplus or waste territory. All had been made to answer the demands of the consumer. Wheat, corn, clover, half a dozen varieties of grass, rye, barley — all in full growth and approaching maturity — met the eye at every turn, all enclosed in rock or strongly and closely built wooden fences. Apples, cherries, currants, pears, quinces, etc., in the utmost profusion, and bee hives *ad infinitum*. The barns were, however, the most striking feature of the landscape, for it was one bright panorama for miles. They invariably occupied the most select building site on the tract, and were equal in size, elegance and finish, and superior in arrangement and adaptation to this purpose to three-fourths of the dwellings in Texas. On the other hand, the dwellings, though neat and comfortable, were secreted in some nook or corner, as if there had been a close calculation that a horse or an ox being the larger animal, required a more spacious residence than a human being. I think the class or position in society must depend somewhat on the size and elegance of the barn.
> The springs and milk houses or dairies were also a noted feature of the country. I think I have seen more than fifty springs equal to those of Barton, San Antonio, San Marcos and Salado. But the most singular phenomenon which impressed me was the scarcity of visible inhabitants, in this apparently densely populated region. Women and children were seen peeping about but as shy as partridges, but in the towns and villages men, women and children thronged by hundreds. I believe two brigades of able bodied men under thirty years of age could have been raised in Chambersburg alone. We were, of

44

course, coldly received everywhere.

On June 15, President Abraham Lincoln called out an additional 100,000 militia over and above that already turned out by the state governors of Pennsylvania and New York. President Lincoln also ordered this militia into national service. Pennsyvlania had at that time about 25 "Emergency" militia regiments under arms. At the June 15 call, the state added eight more, the 20th, 26th, 27th, 28th, 29th, 30th, 31st, and 33rd. Later on June 26 Governor Andrew Curtin made a final plea, and the 32nd, 34th and 60th Regiments were enrolled as "Three Months Men." The previous units were activitated for six months. New York and New Jersey also sent several well-trained regiments to Pennsylvania amounting to an additional twenty or more units totaling over 12,000 men. Pennsylvania had a population of over 3,000,000, which was nearly as many as the whole populace of the Confederacy east of the Mississippi. Yet only about 8,000 Pennsylvania militia were on hand during the campaign to defend their homeland.

3. Colonel Powell means here that men so unused to hard marching were now procuring animals to ease their burdens. This was a normal sight in the early days of a campaign prior to the "toughening up" of the soldier. "Field officers," i.e., colonels, lieutenant colonels, and majors of a regiment, as well as the surgeons and adjutants, were mounted. "Line officers," i.e., captains and lieutentants marched with their companies.

4. Several sources indicate that prior to and during the campaign, hospitals in Richmond and elsewhere did indeed empty out patients who could stand the march and bivouac. During times of bad weather or the inactivity of an army, many soldiers sought out the hospital as a relief from the tedium and boredom of camp life. When the army was put in motion, many of these "bummers" voluntarily left the wards for the excitement and adventure of campaigning. Many of these types, however, were probably useless on the fighting line, and could often be found behind battle lines using every excuse possible to stay out of combat. Soldiers called these men "coffee coolers" as they could usually be found sitting around a small fire in the rear with their hands wrapped around a hot tin of coffee. Of course, many of the men in hospitals *were* legitimately there, and leaving was the ultimate test of comradeship. The marches for this class of fellows must have been torture.

5. Lee's famous General Order #72 dated June 21 and received by the troops three days later forbade looting or any type of "revenge" activities by individual soldiers. Any property taken or destroyed must conform to a regular or controlled process by designated officers of the quartermaster, ordnance, subsistence or medical departments, etc. See the *Official Records*, Vol. 27, Part 3, pp. 912-13 for a transcript of the actual order. Just how was the order obeyed? For one thing, serious acts of incendiarism were rare, as only a handful of houses and barns were destroyed during the Campaign and Battle of Gettysburg. Theft and pillaging and vandalism were more rampant. No rapes were reported, however, some few may have occurred. It was not a subject often spoken of openly in 19th Century America. Any number of examples of looting may be found to give the reader a clear idea of the sheer number of such events. Literally hundreds of examples such as this can be located in the published annals of the battle:

Sunday, July 5th

It appearing evident that the rebels were falling back, our brigade was this morning advanced beyond the line nearly a mile. My company and the sharp shooters of our regiment were under my charge as skirmishers; we encountered nothing but a few of the rebel videttes, but we had a good chance to witness the havoc made by the fire of our artillery during the battle of the 2d. We picked up one hundred good muskets, the rebels having left this line but an hour previous to our advance; and the wrecks of the good things which they had helped themselves to were seen at every step. Fragments of mutton, veal, crocks of butter, lard, preserves, baskets containing delicacies from the cellars of the wealthy farmers in the vicinity, were thickly strewn around. Dressing apparel which could do them no earthly good, such as old bonnets, fashioned after old patterns, babies' shoes, young misses' gaiters, feather beds, in fact everything stealable could be found here in profusion....

The haversacks, knapsacks, and pockets of dead or wounded rebels were found filled with gold watches, jewelry, U.S. currency and coin, and thousands of personal "civilian" articles which had been stolen. There is even an incident near Gettysburg where a Confederate general officer may have made off with thousands in gold. See Gregory Coco, *On The Bloodstained Field II*, p. 47. All of this, of course, was a common fact of life during war time and should not surprise anyone. Almost every soldier sooner or later becomes brutal — and theft and killing and vandalism is commonplace and easy to tolerate after a while. War hardens all concerned; and it has been the same from the Hittites to Americans in Vietnam. In fact, after the battle at Gettysburg thousands of civilians descended onto the battlefield and took everything they could lay their hands on, all of which was government and private property.

Hundreds of farmers and other citizens filed property damage claims after the war with the state and Federal governments. In Adams County alone the loss *reported* in large items was approximately 800 horses, 1,000 head of cattle, a dozen mules, over 200 hogs, over 400 sheep, at least 250 wagons and carriages of all sorts, totaling $552,383. Nearby in Franklin County the loss was nearly 900,000 dollars. This total does *not* count the hundreds and hundreds of acres of growing crops destroyed or taken, or the tons of *stored* produce stolen or damaged, nor does this figure tell of the literally thousands of personal items which were listed in these claims, such as weapons, money, jewelry, clothes, furniture, tools, books, medicines, plows, canned goods, knives, watches, lanterns, toys, butter, harnesses, and hundreds of other items too numerous to mention.

6. Chambersburg, visited at least three times during the war by rebel forces, was a prosperous town of about 5,200 inhabitants, surrounded by 2,496 farms in Franklin County. It had 19 schools, several good hotels, a 20-year-old courthouse valued at $50,000 and many fine churches. There was a railroad through the town, paper mills, *several* tanneries, furniture factories and carriagemakers.

The village was apparently very patriotic to the Union cause. Many Confederates who passed through the town remarked on the dedication of the population to the U.S. government and even to the kindness and generosity of the people. Just over a year later this beautiful village was almost totally destroyed by Confederate raiders.

7. General James E.B. Stuart, commanding Lee's cavalry division, was at this time attempting to make contact with Lee's army, much of which was now in Pennsylvania. Stuart, given much freedom by Lee's orders had chosen to ride eastward around the rear of

the Federal army, scout their whereabouts, then would report the position of the various Union corps to headquarters. However, time had slipped away from Stuart. His scouting abilities, usually so valuable to the Southern commander, were now useless as the cavalry chief, encumbered with a captured wagon train, plodded northward toward Carlisle still looking for a chance to strike southwestward toward the main force of the Confederate army. Stuart finally arrived at General Lee's headquarters west of Gettysburg on July 2, too late to be of much assistance now that the unplanned battle was in progress.

8. A portion of General Ambrose P. Hill's newly organized third corps had brought on the battle early on July 1. Later that day Generals Robert E. Rodes' and Jubal A. Early's Southern divisions of General Richard S. Ewell's second corps struck the Union lines northwest, north and northeast of Gettysburg. These attacks drove the Union army to the hills and ridges south of Gettysburg. General John B. Gordon's brigade was part of Early's division. Total casualties for this brigade were 536, most of which occurred northeast of the town when it overran portions of the Union Eleventh Corps. At this juncture of the battle Powell and his men were farther to the west beyond Marsh Creek and out toward Cashtown.

9. Very few actual "bushwhacking" incidents were recorded during the Gettysburg Campaign. One very detailed story of such an event can be found in the March 13, 1900 edition of the Gettysburg *Compiler,* a local newspaper. The bushwhacker, John Smith, a mountaineer, lived in a log cabin near Cashtown. Reportedly, he had sworn that he would, "shoot the first rebel that came along or die in the event." Evidently, he did just that, as the story related how on Friday, June 26, one of General Jubal Early's men who was in the vanguard of the division, was shot from a "swamp thicket on the north side of the [Chambersburg] pike, some two hundred yards west of what was then the sawmill of the late Daniel Kuhn."*

* This site today is readily visible from U.S. Route 30 West, and is approximately 1½ miles west of Cashtown. The 1872 atlas of Adams County indicates the old location of Daniel Kuhn's house and mill as it stood in 1863.

10. Captain Thomas J. Goree, a member of General James Longstreet's staff from July 23, 1861 to April 9, 1865, would remain a loyal friend to the end of Longstreet's life. The general met him in early 1861 near New Orleans. Goree was described by Longstreet as a "clever, intelligent, Texan," and was considered as one of the most trusted and reliable staff officers of either side during the Civil War, and his integrity was never questioned.

11. The "Devil's Den" area south of Gettysburg was actually part of the property of John Houck, and was on the southern portion of what is called Houck's Ridge. However, the "Den" itself was an actual location, while today that name is incorrectly applied to the entire area of large boulders along that ridge. Colonel John B. Bachelder, the government historian at Gettysburg in the 1890s stated:

> Devil's Den is not a new name; it was a name given to the locality before the battle. It is a gorge, or rather a hole in the ground, and it is difficult to get into it. There is a spring at its mouth, but those big rocks that stand up there are not the Devil's Den.

For additional information on how the Den got its name see Kathleen R.G. Harrison's article, "Our Principal Loss Was In This Place," published in *The Gettysburg Magazine*, issue #1, p. 45, by Morningside Bookshop in July 1989. Ms. Harrison's article is possibly the best research ever done on the fighting of July 2 in that part of the battlefield. Also see Gregory A. Coco, *On The Bloodstained Field II*, Thomas Publications, 1989, p. 7.

12. Captain John S. Cleveland commanded Company H which was organized at Cold Spring, Polk County, Texas, in July 1861. Their local designation was the "Texas Polk Rifles." The records state that he was wounded at Second Manassas and Gettysburg.

Sergeant J.B. Ross of Company H. He was mustered as 1st Corporal in 1861.

Major Jefferson C. Rogers, third in command of the 5th Texas was formerly the captain of Company G, the "Milam County Greys" formed July 15, 1861 at Cameron, Milam County, Texas. Rogers was the only field officer not wounded on July 2, and his report of the battle may be read in Appendix I. He was born in Lawrence County, Tennessee in 1824, and moved to Texas in 1852. His wife was Martha Reed. He was promoted major on November 1, 1862. Rogers was wounded at Chickamauga and retired from the service on October 25, 1864. Later he became a judge in Milam County, and died on February 27, 1885. Rogers was buried in Cameron, Texas.

13. Robert Powell does not go into detail about how he received his wounds, or anything subsequent to his capture, which is unfortunate, because what is left out may be the most interesting part of all. Lieutenant Colonel King Bryan does give a good description of the immediate situation in his report which the reader may examine in Appendix I. Colonel Joshua L. Chamberlain, 20th Maine Infantry, mentions Powell in a narrative of the fight at Little Round Top written in Hearst's Magazine about 1913. As the 20th began clearing the area in their front and right Chamberlain said:

> Ranks were broken; many retired before us somewhat hastily; some threw their muskets to the ground — even loaded; sunk on ther knees, threw up their hands, calling out, 'We surrender. Don't kill us!' As if we wanted to do that! We kill only to resist killing. And these were manly men, whom we would befriend, and by no means kill, if they came our way in peace and good will. Charging right through and over these, we struck the second line of the Forty-seventh Alabama doing their best to stand, but offering little resistance. Their Lieutenant-Colonel as I passed — and a fine gentleman was Colonel Bulger — introduced himself as my prisoner, and as he was wounded, I had him cared for as best we could. Still swinging to the right as a great gate on its hinges, we swept the front clean of assailants. We were taking in prisoners by scores — more than we could hold, or sent to the rear, so that many made final escape up Great Round Top. Half way down to the throat of the vale I came upon Colonel Powell of the Fourth Alabama, [sic] a man of courtly bearing, who was badly wounded. I sent him to the Eighty-third Pennsylvania, nearest to us and better able to take care of him than we were.

The 83rd Pennsylvania did indeed end up with Powell. One member had a slightly different reaction to that Texas colonel than did Chamberlain. Amos M. Judson recalled:

> The rebel forces engaged on this occasion were principally Alabama and Texas troops. Several of the prisoners boasted that this was the first time they

had ever been whipped. Among the prominent prisoners were Colonel Bulger, and a Colonel Powell. Bulger was a small, bald headed man, apparently between fifty and sixty, and had formerly been a member of Congress from Texas. He had received a severe wound, I think in the breast, and spoke and acted as if he was evidently tired of the war. He was pleasant and courteous in his manners and conversation, and this moved in us a feeling of strong sympathy for his suffering. As I sat and looked upon that deluded old gentleman, who had once occupied the proud and comfortable position of a member of the Congress of the United States, now lying at midnight upon the bare ground, with nothing to shield his aged and shivering limbs from the cold, his wound gaping and his frame writhing in the tortures of that wound, afar from his family and children — I could not but reflect upon his folly in this his attempt to overthrow the government of his fathers and to engage in the vain pursuit of military glory. The other Colonel, Powell, was a man of quite a different stamp. He was one of your morose, sullen men, who imagine that to be insolent in the hour of defeat and humiliation is to be brave and resolute. 'You have peppered us pretty badly,' he observed with an air of self-satisfaction to Captain [O. S.] Woodward, 'but you'll get the worst of it before it's over!' He had been wounded in the breast and was sent back to the hospital where the other rebel wounded lay. It was afterwards reported that he attempted to get up a conspiracy among the rebel wounded at the hospital, and was sent to Washington in chains. For the truth of this story, however, I cannot vouch.

"Captain White" presented a very difficult problem as to his identification. The only captain that I found by that name who was *possibly* anywhere in the vicinity of Little Round Top on the afternoon of July 2 was Captain John R. White, 118th Pennsylvania Infantry. Since the 118th was engaged nearer to the "Wheatfield," it was unlikely he is our man. It is unfortunate that Powell did not give a first name, and in fact "White" may have been incorrect. For now, at least, this "Captain White" must remain a mystery, and his exciting story of bravery may never be acknowledged.

Colonel Michael Jefferson Bulger was born in 1806 in Richmond District, South Carolina. In 1823 he moved to Montgomery, Alabama. Commissioned Captain of Company A, 47th Alabama on March 20, 1862, at Gettysburg he served as lieutenant colonel of that regiment. Made prisoner at the battle, he was exchanged in March of 1864. Bulger died in 1900, his sword still in the possession of a member of the 83rd., O.W. Norton.

14. In consulting Ed Raus' excellent reference book entitled, *A Generation on the March — The Union Army at Gettysburg*, I came across only one regiment which served in the Gettysburg Campaign and was from Rochester, New York. In fact, its "nickname" was the "Rochester Regiment." This unit was the 8th New York Cavalry and its commander at Gettysburg was Lieutenant Colonel William Lester Markell, a 26 year old who was a manufacturer and wholesaler in that city before the war. Was Colonel Markell the elusive "Dare Devil Dick?" There is no positive way to be sure. No other officer of any New York Cavalry unit at Gettysburg had the first name "Richard" which would have possibly narrowed the field somewhat. Colonel Markell was wounded on July 10, 1863, was mustered out of service on February 27, 1864 and died in 1916.

In another story dealing with the city of Rochester, a soldier of the 140th New York,

Corporal James R. Campbell wrote a letter some time just after the battle of July 2nd near Little Round Top. The following is quoted from his manuscript:

> The Regiment which we drove back was the 5th Texas. After the fight a Lieutenant of our Regiment came to me and told me that a Rochester boy (a prisoner taken by us when we charged) wanted to see me. I thought this kind of strange but in the afternoon, having a little time, I went down to see my pretended acquaintance, and who should I meet but Ben Simpson. He was very glad to see me. He says he will try and get paroled, and go home and see the folks, and then join the Rebels again; but I think if he gets home he can be induced to stay. We took his colonel and a great number of his Regiment prisoners. He says, and his Colonel confirms it, that we are the only Regiment that ever defeated them. He hopes that our Regiment may never meet his again, but that if it does he will turn over and fire the other way.

Another man of the 140th also recalled the incident. He said:

> With their wounded we found a Rochester boy, who had been in the rebel service for some time past, and I am shamed to say thinks it an honor to him to be fighting for Southern Rights! (Have traitors any rights?) I am glad that the number of Rochester boys so lost to all self respect is remarkably small. His name is Benjamin Simpson, and he belonged to the 5th Texas Regiment. He was impressed in the service at Galveston, and has since become, by association, thoroughly saturated with secesh. He feels proud of the brigade to which he was attached, and says they never failed to carry any point they were ordered to.

My appreciation goes to Brian A. Bennett of Scottsville, New York, for this unusual and interesting sidelight of the battle.

15. The paragraph above mentions two brothers, meeting each other at Gettysburg. During my research I have found at least three similar accounts of this phenomenon. Two brothers on opposing sides met on July 1 near Oak Ridge; similarly two met in rear of the Christ Lutheran Church on Chambersburg Street in Gettysburg. And there is the one noted by Powell, of course. There are many other accounts of brothers on the *same* side meeting each other at Gettysburg, and even one man meeting his sister in a hospital after the battle. For more information, see Gregory A. Coco, *On The Bloodstained Field, Vols. I and II.*

The 14th United States Infantry was part of General R.B. Ayres' 2nd Division, Fifth Army Corps. It consisted of eight companies and its strength at Gettysburg was 601, with losses of 18 killed, 110 wounded, and 4 missing. The regiment was enlisted in New York City and around Providence, R.I., Onondaga, N.Y., and Chemung, N.Y. The commander was Major G.R. Giddings. The 14th fought about several hundred yards north of where Powell's Texans struck the base of Little Round Top. However, one officer in the 11th U.S. Infantry, Lieutenant James Pratt, which was in the same battalion as the 14th, said in a letter written to his father on July 13:

> The long ridge, that was on our flank, was crowded with Texan sharpshooters, who did terrible work. They were lying down. All I could see of them was the flash of their rifles along the ridge, and the 'Lone Star' flag in the centre of it.

So it is partially true that Powell "met" the 14th on his "bloody excursion up Little Round Top."

16. This rumor of the possible retreat of General George G. Meade began purely by accident some time after 11 a.m. on July 2. Chief of Staff General Daniel Butterfield had supposedly been directed by Meade to draw up a contingency plan to be used in case the army was forced to retreat from Gettysburg. Butterfield purposefully or not, may have spread the rumor that Meade planned to retreat. In any case that notion flashed throughout the Army of the Potomac, and eight months later Meade had to appear before a "committee on the conduct of the war" to answer charges that he intended to retreat during the battle. It is doubtful that this was ever the general's intention, but regardless the whole question became an embarrassment to Meade. For more information on this interesting question, see p. 338 in E.B. Coddington's *The Gettysburg Campaign.*

17. Another rumor which cropped up during the battle and was believed by many officers and men was that General George B. McClellan was on his way to the battlefield to take command of the Union army. Many contemporary accounts verify that this belief was rampant throughout the army. Even the Confederates had heard it. Of course, there was no truth to it, but the rumors persisted. In fact, before the opening days of the campaign many prominent citizens and politicians of both parties in the North began to worry that the populace and army needed a more charismatic leader, such as General McClellan. And as the invasion became a reality and Lee swept deeper into the states of Maryland and Pennsylvania, louder and louder went the call for a change of leadership. Therefore it can readily be seen why throughout this period many in the army began to believe the rumors. It is even possible that to instill confidence in the Union army, many who still loved McClellan perpetuated the talk of his impending arrival on purpose.

18. The "stone house" mentioned by Colonel Powell may have been the house of Sarah and Jacob Weikert who lived on a 102 acre farm in rear of the Round Tops. Ironically the house stood almost exactly 1,000 yards east/southeast of the area where Colonel Powell was wounded and found by the 20th Maine. So there is a great possibiliy that he was eventually removed to a section of this farm "among some large rocks." In fact the mention of U.S. Regulars being at this field hospital is another sound clue, because the Jacob Weikert house was a hospital for a portion of Ayres' Regular Division of the Fifth Corps. See p. 68, Gregory A. Coco, *A Vast Sea of Misery — A History and Guide to the Union and Confederate Field Hospitals at Gettysburg.*

Jacob, 66, and Sarah Weikert, 61, had at least three children; Rebecca, 19, David, 14, and an older married son, Emmanuel. One officer who visited the Weikert's farm during the battle, Lieutenant Ziba B. Graham, 16th Michigan Infantry, stated:

> On my way back to the regiment the fighting commenced upon the right of the line. It was the most terrific artillery firing that was ever heard upon this continent. Our corps was not engaged in this battle, although many of the shells fell in its midst. We were maintaining the line just to the left of where Pickett's Charge came in contact with our centre. On my way back to rejoin the regiment I called at a large house for a drink of water; I saw that the well crank had been removed. I turned to a rebel captain who was lying on the grass and asked him if he knew where it had gone to; he said the owner of the house

had taken it off, declaring he was not going to have his well pumped dry by rebel soldiers, and that they wasted the water. This captain begged that I might get it again. There were some fifty rebel wounded in the yard, besides a few of our own men. The surgeons who had been with them, and who had partly gone around in their first examination, had cleared out and left them on the commencement of the firing, and with the fever of their gunshot wounds they were thirsting for water. I went into the house, found this man, a mean Dutchman, buried in the bosom of his family, and his family buried in the bowels of the cellar, they having taken safe refuge from the hail of iron which was bursting in every direction. I ordered him to give up the well crank. He first refused. Just at that time a shell struck his chimney, and the noise and rattle of the falling brick nearly frightened him to death. I threatened to shoot him if he did not give me the crank; this brought it out of its hiding place back of the stairway. I went out, watered the boys, put two of the least wounded in charge of it and then left, receiving the thanks of all.

Every visit I have since made to Little Round Top, I have seen "old Wikerts" son — his father is now dead — telling interested hearers of "the wonderful acts of heroism his father and he did in taking care of the wounded in their yard that fearful day, and how kind the government was to recognize their services.

19. There is *some* truth to this paragraphs's statement. Troops in the rear — no matter what their function i.e., quartermaster, medical, provost marshal, or plain old "deserters," did receive a terrible pounding from Confederate artillery, much of which in the 1½ hour bombardment preceding "Pickett's Charge" did overshoot its intended mark. In fact damage was so severe to the hospitals in the rear, that many along the Taneytown Road were forced to move further to the southeast and nearer to Rock Creek and the Baltimore Turnpike. The cannonade did not generally cause troops to rush to the front in great numbers as Powell supposes. In point of fact, the provost marshal of the Army of the Potomac, General M.R. Patrick, stated:

Friday, 3 July —

I never saw such artillery fire as came upon us at one time. It was terrific & I had my hands full with those who broke to the rear, but we succeeded in checking the disorder & organized a guard of stragglers to keep nearly 2,000 Prisoners all safe.

20. The scene around the Weikert farm must have been both terrible and sublime, but at least two surgeons stated that by 9 o'clock a.m. on July 3 the hospital, which was that of the 2nd Division, Fifth Army Corps, had already begun to be moved. The order had come down from General George Sykes, commander of the Fifth Corps, at about 5 or 6 a.m. on Friday morning (July 3). About 9 o'clock a.m. Surgeon Clinton Wagner who was the surgeon-in-chief of the division just mentioned, remembered:

Between 8 and 9 o'clock on Friday....shells [began to fall] not only in the hospital but went beyond and fell dangerously near the ambulance train....One shell fell near the operating table at which I was performing an amputation of the thigh.

During the shelling, which did not last but a few minutes, the hospital staff, as was expected, remained at their posts, exhibiting neither fear nor excitement. The removal of the wounded lasted until sunset.

Another surgeon, Dr. John S. Billings, also of the 2nd Division, reported:

On July 3 at 7:00 o'clock a.m., I was ordered by Surgeon [John J.] Milhau medical director of the corps, to remove the hospital [from the Weikert house] to a point about one mile to the rear. This was done as rapidly as possible. A few shells began to drop in as the first train of ambulances moved off, and by 11:00 o'clock a.m. the fire on that point was quite brisk.

Therefore it is possible that the 1 o'clock to 3 o'clock p.m. bombardment caught Powell and other wounded still in place at the Weikert farm, with but a few medical attendants for company and aid.

21. Colonel Powell is very accurate when he mentions that "surgeons and attendants were distressingly slow in making their appearance." The sad fact was, that over 26,000 men were wounded in the three-day battle at Gettysburg. Even by modern standards it would have been very difficult for a present day U.S. medical establishment to administer properly to that many wounded in so short a period of time. And since Powell and thousands of Confederate wounded were in Union hands they often had to wait until the Northern soldier who had been injured was cared for first. Nearly all of the medical trains were left behind as Meade's army toiled toward Gettysburg, with only the Sixth Corps (which was not heavily engaged) having medical supplies nearby. It took several days to get these important items to the field, and a week to ten days before real relief began to be felt by the vast sea of wounded. Actually Powell was very lucky to receive aid as quickly as he did.

22. During my years researching material on the Battle of Gettysburg I have found several accounts where soldiers committed suicide during or after the battle. Obviously it was a more common occurrence than one would care to imagine. These incidents happened in all wars when pain, desperation, serious wounds, loss of mental facilities or disillusionment would cause a man to seek a final solution to any or all of these horrible problems. For one such account see *On The Bloostained Field*, p. 28. In that story Captain J.A. Moore, 147th Pennsylvania, witnesses a wounded rebel soldier who deliberately shot himself through the head.

23. More than one visitor to the field verified this interesting occurrence where a cannon was plugged at the muzzle. One gun, which has since become famous and is now on exhibit at the State House in Providence, Rhode Island, was a 12-pounder which became plugged when it was being loaded. The muzzle was deformed after being struck by a Confederate cannon ball, and was also very hot. When the new ball to be fired was placed into the barrel opening, it would not go to the bottom of the tube. As the gun cooled the bronze barrel contracted around the cannon ball where it remains today.

Several other tubes were probably struck by shells or solid shot fired by opposing batteries. This happened at least once when an Ohio battery accurately disabled a Confederate gun nearly ½ mile away with a shot directly into the muzzle. For several other witnesses to these unusual sights, see *On The Bloodstained Field II*, p. 33.

24. During my research on a book about the wounded and field hospitals at Gettysburg I came across 68 actual references by Union and Confederate soldiers of the kindness or total disregard shown by this particular class of people. The overwhelming vote came out about 50 to 1 *against* the typical *Adams County* resident for his seemingly selfish and uncaring attitude toward the soldiers who fought in the battle, many of whom were seriously wounded. On the other hand, the residents of the *borough of Gettysburg proper* were given just the opposite vote. Most who came in contact with the townsfolk found them very helpful and kind to a fault. Of course, it is very unfair to make generalized statements, and this is not intended to be critical. See p. 45 of *On The Bloodstained Field II* and p. 41 in *Vol. I* for more on the attitudes of the Adams County farmers, or various references in *A Vast Sea of Misery*, all by Gregory A. Coco.

25. By the 6th of July most military units had left the Gettysburg area. Some units of U.S. regulars were ordered to New York City to help quell the draft riots there and to keep peace. Others were now with Meade's Army of the Potomac following Lee's army which was now in full retreat toward the relative safety of Virginia.

Left behind were details of provost guards, 106 surgeons and several hundred medical attendants, plus various quartermaster people who were attempting to clean up the battlefield. Over 21,000 wounded remained behind, thousands of corpses of men and several thousands of horses and mules killed or seriously injured in the battle. Before it was all over nearly 10,000 men would die as a result of the three-day engagement. Many of the wounded remained in hospitals around Gettysburg until December 1, 1863. The Confederate dead would remain longer — at least until 1871 — 73 when about 3,400 were exhumed and removed for reburial in the South. Many of the Union dead, of course, would eventually be reinterred in the new Soldiers' National Cemetery dedicated on November 19, 1863.

26. Andrew Gregg Curtin was forty-six and had served as governor of Pennsylvania since 1860. He is considered to be one of the best governors in the commonwealth's history. A staunch supporter of Lincoln's policies, Curtin helped to raise over 427,000 troops for U.S. service during the war, and was a strong friend of the common soldier. Curtin visited the battlefield about the middle of July and toured various hospitals in and near Gettysburg during that time. He was elected to a second term in 1864. After the war he ran for Congress where he served three terms. Andrew Curtin died in 1894.

One other soldier who recalled the governor's visit was Jacob Shenkel, a private in the 62nd Pennsylvania Infantry. On Saturday, July 11, Shenkel noted in his diary:

> J.K. MoreHead & Governor Curtin visited the wounded to Day. they Did Not Remain Long. J.K. was after His Son. He was wounded at the battle....

Private Shenkel was acting as nurse in the 1st Division, Fifth Corps hospital. This is logical as Colonel Powell was in the hospital of the Fifth Corps for awhile. It is possible that when Powell saw Curtin he was then at the Michael Fiscel farm which was about 1½ miles southeast of Weikert's.

27. Robert Powell's saga of an impersonation of Lieutenant General James Longstreet makes for an interesting story. Several sources reported the "facts" of the situation. General E.M. Law, one of Longstreet's brigade commanders, wrote:

> ...some of ours [prisoners] remained in their [U.S.] hands in the most

advanced positions which we had reached and had been compelled to abandon. Among these latter was Colonel Powell of the 5th Texas regiment who was shot through the body....Powell was a stout, portly man, with a full beard, resembling, in many rspects, General Longstreet, and the first impression of his captors was that they had taken that officer. Indeed, it was asserted positively by some of the prisoners we picked up during the night that Longstreet was badly wounded and a prisoner in their hands, and they obstinately refused to credit our statements to the contrary.

A Union officer, Captain John D.S. Cook, 80th New York Infantry, recalled the confusion resulting in the supposed "Longstreet capture."

[I rode] past the house where General Meade had established headquarters. He rode up with his staff as I came along. I heard him inquiring about the report that General Longstreet had been killed and told him I had just come from the front with a captured officer of Pickett's division and that the report was current that General Longstreet had been killed under one of our guns at the head of the charge. He doubted whether the report could be true and remarked that "Any army must be in a desperate condition when a corps commander led a charge like that." His instinct was right. The charge was led by a General officer who fell at our guns and died in a few minutes. Before he died he gave his name as General Armistead. Some of the men near him thought he said "Longstreet" and the report quickly spread that the famous corps commander had fallen. It was this mistaken report which I had heard and repeated to General Meade who readily showed its improbability.

A visitor to the battlefield on July 7, John B. Linn, also heard about the "death" of Longstreet and the resulting confusion. So, obviously the story already was common knowledge in the army and the civilian community.

Linn said in his diary:

Mr. Bucher explained the mistake in regard to the report of Longstreet's death, that Gen. Armistead's death was signaled to Headquarters Armstreath. As they knew no Armstreath they concluded it must mean Longstreet.

28. The Pennsylvania College main building was built between 1836 and 1837 and was the earliest building to be erected on the campus of that college. During most of its years it served as a dormitory.

While the battle was in progress and for several weeks afterwards (until July 29) it was used as a field hospital for men of General Jubal Early's Confederate division. There were anywhere from 700 to 900 patients in this hospital, and 35 soldiers who died there were buried just north of the building.

The edifice was 3½ stories high and 150 feet in length topped by a 24 foot high cupola and was built on land which had once belonged to Thaddeus Stevens.

29. The college president, Henry L. Baugher, was born in 1804 and died in 1868. He became president of the institution in 1850, but had been a teacher and faculty member since 1832. During the battle Baugher and his family lived in a brick house on the campus which was very near the main edifice, and was one of only three buildings standing in that year.

Henry Baugher was also one of the volunteer ministers who conducted services at the Christ Lutheran Church on Chambersburg Street.

Even after consulting the 1860 census records and other sources in the Adams County Historical Society it was still very difficult to determine who the "ten-year-old boy" mentioned by Powell, actually was. In 1863, Baugher did not have a son that age. His youngest was Witmer, who was 17. However, Professor Michael Jacobs who lived in Gettysburg at the corner of Washington and Middle Streets, did have a son, George, who was nine, almost ten, in that year. Dr. Charles Glatfelter of the Society noted that since Jacobs was on the college faculty, as professor of mathematics and natural science, it seemed possible that Powell, after so many years, may have forgotten who actually visited him. Jacobs' son, George would have been ten by late 1863. Professor Jacobs was 52 and married to Julia, 48. They had one other son, Michael W., who was 13. Jacobs was very interested in the battle and probably spent many hours on the campus in those long summer days. Subsequently, Jacobs wrote several articles, etc., on Gettysburg and its place in history.

Returning to Henry Baugher; the reader may be interested to note that one of his elder sons had been killed in 1862 as a result of the battle of Shiloh, Tennessee, yet he and his wife, Clarissa, did everything in their power to aid both Union and Confederate wounded who occupied their house as well as the main college building.

30. This "Dr. Groves" presented a perplexing problem, as my research uncovered no Southerner by that name who died of wounds or disease while at Gettysburg. If in fact Dr. Groves was the surgeon of a Mississippi regiment, I was unable to verify that information. Therefore, for the time being he must remain anonymous.

31. As the reader may recall from the quoted material in Note #13, Powell himself *was* suspected of plotting an escape from Union hands at Gettysburg. In fact several Confederates did make good their flight from the field with the aid of sympathizers from Maryland and elsewhere. In some cases civilian clothes were smuggled to the rebels who then simply walked off. For an account of two soldiers who did this, see *On The Bloodstained Field*, p. 42.

One nurse who reportedly aided Confederates in eluding the Federal army at Gettysburg was Euphemia Mary Goldsborough who was posted as a nurse at the "College Hospital." Her ward consisted of 50 Union and 50 Confederate wounded. She resided on Courtland Street in Baltimore and was a fervent secessionist. After her work at the college, "Effie" Goldsborough was sent to Camp Letterman, one mile east of Gettysburg where she assisted the wounded there for several months before returning home. If she in fact, aided in any escapes while at Gettysburg, charges were never forthcoming. Oddly, of all the soldiers Mrs. Goldsborough nursed, a favorite was Sam H. Watson, Co. E, 5th Texas, one of Colonel Powell's men who had an arm amputated and later died in "Effie's" arms. The letter to Sam's mother telling of his fate, "nearly broke her heart."

One infamous temporary resident of the College Edifice was Lewis T. Powell, 2nd Florida Infantry, who was wounded during Pickett's Charge on July 3. This Rebel private was cared for, then sent to a prison in Baltimore where he escaped and returned to the C.S. Army in Virginia. Later Private Powell deserted and changed his name to Lewis Payne, where he joined the conspirators under John Wilkes Booth. Payne's part of the plot involved the murder of Secretary of State W.H. Steward, which he failed to accomplish. He was hanged in 1865.

32. Dr. James K. Shivers, U.S. Volunteer surgeon, was stationed after the battle both at the College and at Camp Letterman General Hospital where he worked with the wounded for several months. On July 26, Dr. Lennox Hodge was reported to be in charge at the College Hospital. There may have been a Confederate surgeon there also, Dr. H.D. Fraser of South Carolina, as well as a Dr. "Smiley" who was a member of Heth's Division.

Shivers, mentioned above, could not be located in any of the standard references on the Civil War, such as *The Official Army Register of the Volunteer Force of the U.S. Army*, by F.B. Heitman, nor did he appear in *The Official Records of the War of the Rebellion*, so any personal information on the doctor must regrettably be left out of this entry.

33. Unfortunately, "Miss E." must remain another mystery. Evidently, she was a school-teacher and *not* a nurse, for there were several nurses at Gettysburg who had an "E" for the first letter in their last names. There was C.A. Elher from Lancaster, PA; Mrs. D. Eagerton of Baltimore, MD; also Ms. Susan A. Edson; Ms. Elizabeth Ewing; Ms. Anna Etheridge; and Ms. Annie P. Erving, none of which fit the description of the teacher noted by Powell.

34. The Lutheran Theological Seminary had been established on a ridge just west of Gettysburg in the 1820s. Three buildings stood on that famous ridge in 1863, the main building, which housed the students and classrooms was the structure to which Powell was brought. This large building had become a field hospital on July 1 and remained so well into late August. The three-and-one-half story brick structure was completed in 1832 and was 100 x 40 feet. Today it houses the Adams County Historical Society and is one of the most beautiful and tasteful buildings standing anywhere in the county. From the cupola, several officers were able to direct or make battle plans during the battle. For more information on this place as a field hospital, see *A Vast Sea of Misery*, p. 6.

Several physicians who did medical work at the Lutheran Seminary hospital were Dr. Henry Leaman, an acting assistant surgeon; Dr. Andrew J. Ward, 2nd Wisconsin Infantry; Dr. William F. Osborne, 11th Pennsylvania Infantry; Dr. George W. New, 7th Indiana Infantry; and Dr. Robert Loughran, 80th New York Infantry.

35. Isaac R. Trimble was born in Culpeper County, Virginia in 1802 and graduated from the United States Military Academy at West Point in 1822. In August 1861 he was appointed brigadier general in the Confederate Army. Trimble was seriously wounded at Second Manassas and did not rejoin the army until late June of 1863 just prior to the Battle of Gettysburg. On July 3 while leading Pender's division in the attack on Cemetery Ridge he suffered a wound which resulted in the loss of his leg. After recuperating he began a long stay in Federal prison, and was discharged in 1865, Trimble did not rejoin the army. The 85-year-old former Confederate officer died in Baltimore in 1888.

James L. Kemper was born in Madison County, Virginia in 1823, and years later graduated from Washington College. He subsequently became a lawyer and in 1846 joined a Virginia unit during the Mexican War. Kemper also served as a member of the state house of delegates. In 1861 he was commissioned colonel of the 7th Virginia Infantry, and was promoted to brigadier general in 1862. At Gettysburg General Kemper led a brigade in Pickett's division where he was seriously wounded and captured on July 3. Exchanged in 1864, he remained on duty in the defenses of Richmond. After the war Kemper served as governor of Virginia from 1874 to 1877. He died in 1895.

36. Henry K. Douglas was born in Shepherdstown, Virginia on September 29, 1840. He

attended Franklin and Marshall College in Lancaster, Pennsylvania, from which he graduated in 1859. Douglas next studied law at a private school in Lexington, Virginia and was admitted to the bar in 1860.

In late April, 1861, he joined Company B, 2nd Virginia Infantry as a private. In this company Douglas rose to lieutenant, then to captain. In time he joined the staff of General Thomas J. Jackson and served in that status until "Stonewall's" death in May 1863. Promoted to colonel he served on the staffs of Generals Edward Johnson, John B. Gordon, Jubal A. Early, J.H. Pegram and John A. Walker. At one point Douglas commanded the 13th and 49th Virginia regiments. During the war he was wounded six times. After Gettysburg, Henry Douglas was sent to a hospital in Baltimore then on to Johnson's Island prison in Ohio where he spent the winter of 1863-4. On March 18, 1864, he was paroled and exchanged and some weeks afterwards was given command of the "Light Brigade" in Lee's army, which he led until Appomattox, where his unit was the last to stack arms on April 9.

After the war, Douglas resumed the practice of law in Winchester, Virginia, and Hagerstown, Maryland, where he died of tuberculosis in 1903.

37. Jack Howard, like many of the characters "lightly" identified in Powell's reminiscenses, must remain unknown. The "red breeches zouaves" mentioned may refer to the 84th New York Infantry or "Fourteenth Militia" or "Brooklyn Chasseurs" which was one unit that wore zouave-type red trousers. This regiment was organized at Fort Green in Brooklyn, New York, in 1861, and was led at Gettysburg by Colonel Edward B. Fowler and fought on July 1 just west of the Seminary. Their losses were 13 killed and 105 wounded and 99 missing. It may be possible that Howard was detailed as hospital attendant at the Seminary Hospital which was where some of the 84th's wounded men were taken.

NOTES TO EPILOGUE

1. Robert K. Krick. *Lee's Colonels,* op cit., p. 265.

2. Simpson, Harold B. *Hood's Texas Brigade in Reunion and Memory.* Hill Junior College Press, Hillsboro, Texas, 1974, p. 63.

INDEX

PART II

"My Gettysburg Battle Experiences,"
by Capt. George Hillyer, 9th Georgia Infantry, C.S.A.

Acknowledgments

The editor would like to thank the following individuals for their generosity and assistance in making this publication possible. They are: Julie Chavez, Cindy L. Small, Mary Robinson, Brion FitzGerald, Bernard W. Wolff, Greg C. White, Curt Musselman, Paul Shevchuk, Charlotte Ray, John Heiser, Troy Harman, Scott Hartwig, Katy Stowe, Andie Custer, Tim Orr, and John Griffin's Internet site, *The Ninth Georgia Infantry, CSA.*

About this book

The Gettysburg recollections of Captain George Hillyer are unique and interesting for several reasons. His account, although composed many years after the events took place, is benefited not only by Hillyer's natural intellect, but also by his occupation as a distinguished lawyer and judge. Furthermore, although only a captain in rank, it was Hillyer who commanded the 9th Georgia in the great battle. So, within days of the engagement, he drew up for Confederate authorities the regiment's official report of the action. And as an added bonus, his post-war narrative and official report are enhanced and supported by yet another excellent source: a long and detailed letter written to his father on July 11 highlighting his battlefield adventures. But there is another enjoyable feature of Hillyer's memoir, and that is the engaging style in which he related it. Instead of presenting simply a general overview, he decided to tell his regiment's story by using the element of human interest. Therefore, the reader sees the battle through the eyes of the common soldier, rather than from the impersonal observations of the high command, or of a latter day historian. Finally, the fact that Hillyer's unit was involved in some of the most intensely critical and dangerous combat at Gettysburg, only adds to his exciting and mesmerizing tale. These combined circumstances make Captain Hillyer's experiences simply one of the best military sources to have emerged from that historical event.[1]

*Anderson's Brigade marker along Seminary Ridge on the
Gettysburg battlefield.*

My Gettysburg Battle Experiences

By Captain George Hillyer, 9th Georgia Infantry, C.S.A.

In the early spring months of 1863, General James Longstreet was engaged in military operations around Suffolk, Virginia and the adjacent counties of North Carolina. All the Federals in that region were hemmed in at Suffolk and Norfolk. Immense supplies were gathered from the rich territory in that part of North Carolina, the supplies to be used by the Army of Northern Virginia in the coming summer campaign.[2] Longstreet had with him General John B. Hood's Division, of Georgia, Alabama and Texas, and some Virginia and North Carolina troops, with cavalry and artillery.[3]

The battle of Chancellorsville occurred some 200 miles distant during this period, and in this way it happened that the part of the army, Hood's Division and General George Anderson's Brigade, to which we belonged, missed the Chancellorsville fight.[4]

Shortly afterwards, however, when the immense wagon trains had carried great quantities of grain and forage out of Gates and other North Carolina counties, as well as countless numbers of cattle, Longstreet withdrew from Suffolk, and with his entire command marched through Richmond by way of Frederick Hall and Orange Court House, joining General Robert E. Lee at Culpepper. We were here when the last preparations for the Pennsylvania campaign were made, and after some weeks of maneuvering and skirmishing, during which every Yankee was driven out, and across the Rappahannock River, Lee's army moved by the left flank up the valley of the Rappahannock, over the Blue Ridge, through the Shenandoah and Cumberland Valleys, across western Maryland, and into Pennsylvania, Longstreet's Corps principally concentrating at Chambersburg, Pennsylvania.[5]

General J.E.B. Stuart's cavalry in the meantime, having crossed the Rappahannock in front of Culpepper, moved to near Manassas and threatened Washington City, then passed between the Yankee army and Washington, crossing the Potomac River through Loudoun County; likewise passing through Maryland, keeping to the right of Lee's main line of march, but with the entire Federal army between him and Lee. Stuart, during this march, tore up the railroads, destroyed the bridges and a canal, burned the enemy's wagon trains, and captured more prisoners that he could keep, getting rid of them by parole.

In the meantime, General Richard Ewell, commanding Stonewall Jackson's old corps, having crossed the Potomac at Harper's Ferry, had made his way into Pennsylvania far to the east of Longstreet's column. Ewell had with him what was left of Jackson's old and tried lieutenants, among them John B. Gordon. Ewell's corps penetrated as far as, and occupied York and Carlisle, and his cavalry appeared on the banks of the Susquehanna River in sight of Harrisburg, the capital of Pennsylvania.

During the movements of our infantry columns, and of the cavalry above mentioned, many small combats and battles, involving only parts of the army, though sometimes as much as two or three divisions, occurred. In these operations the Confederates were nearly always successful, sometimes triumphant, and overwhelmingly so, such as the capture of Union General Robert Milroy with six thousand prisoners at Winchester.[6]

During our occupancy of Pennsylvania territory, private rights were universally respected. The people of Pennsylvania were as safe in their homes, their persons and property, whilst the country was occupied by Lee's Army, as was any territory in the South within the Confederate lines.

Suddenly, after the part of the army to which we belonged had enjoyed a few days rest near Chambersburg, news came that a battle was going on at Gettysburg, some twenty-nine miles distant, and east of Chambersburg. Such an event had evidently been anticipated, for our men had been supplied with extra ammunition and rations.

With the readiness and precision acquired by veterans, we took the road for the scene of conflict, about two o'clock in the afternoon of July 1, 1863. A long range of mountains intervened, and the road was more or less encumbered by artillery and ordinance trains. But we marched as rapidly as possible, and an hour before daylight arrived within a mile or so of the scene of battle. Here Hood's Division halted, and lying down upon the ground we slept on our arms until after daylight, when the march was renewed, and the division deployed on the field. General Henry Benning's Brigade was on the right of the division, and Anderson's on the left, both of these being Georgians. General Evander Law's Alabamians and Jerome Robertson's Texans were in the center, making in all four brigades.

There was no actual fighting going on at the moment, except between the skirmishers of the two armies who were in full view before us, our division being drawn up along the crest of Seminary Ridge. The enemy's lines occupied Cemetery Ridge and Cemetery Hill about three quarters of a mile off. We could see Round Top two or three miles to the right, it being the enemy's left, and to which Cemetery Ridge held by them extended.[7]

Whilst our division was resting in this position, the long lines of infantry reclining in the clover of the open fields with the wooded land on the crest of Seminary Ridge in our rear, General Lee, just after sunrise approached the field. Turning to the right, he took a position under a spreading tree, and sitting on a gray war-horse, took out his glass and began a survey of the field. His staff was with him, grouped some twenty yards in the rear. He had passed our column during the night, but in the dark, we could not well distinguish him. When sitting there on his horse, he was in plain view, not more than sixty yards from my regiment. I remember the idea came into my mind that it would be wonderful and almost sublime could anyone see and know the momentous ideas that were passing through his brain. One of the men in my company well expressed it by an epigram of a kind not uncommon among the men of a veteran army. He said, "Boys there are ten thousand men sitting on that one horse," meaning the Confederacy could better spare ten thousand others, than that one man. After a little while a group of general officers rode up from the wooded land in the rear, and General Lee rode back and met them. We afterwards learned that the celebrated correspondent of the London *Times*, and possibly an eminent officer of the Prussian Army was in the group, but we could distinctly recognize Generals Longstreet and Hood among the number.[8]

During this time, we could see the frowning batteries of the enemy on Cemetery Ridge. There was a friend of mine, Lieutenant Frederick Bliss of the 8th Georgia, whom it had been my honor and my pleasure to befriend under some trying circumstances. In a former campaign, I was Judge Advocate of a court-martial, and Bliss had been on trial charged with having left the ranks during a battle without permission and without necessity. He was prosecuted quite vigorously, but upon investigating the facts, I became satisfied that his conduct was caused by illness, genuine and serious, and that he was a gentleman, gallant and brave, not guilty of the charge. I determined that he should not be convicted or punished. I advised the court to acquit him, and it was done. Often after this, when on the march, he would get permission and leave his command, and walk by my side. I found his presence and talk charming, and his sentiments noble. On this occasion, he came to where I was lying down on the clover, and joined me, resting his head on my knee.

Just then, someone, pointing across the valley to the Federal batteries on the hill beyond, spoke like this: "Now boys, we are going to have a great battle and a great victory today. Suppose that by divine revelation, it was made known in a manner that we all believed it, that if one of us would walk across that valley and up to those batteries and be blown to atoms by one of those cannon, and thus sacrificing one life instead of many, the victory would be ours. Is there one of us that could do it?" I was just beginning to examine my own mind, and to wonder whether I would be equal to the task, but before the hasty thought found expression, Bliss rose up, and with his eye beaming, pointed his finger to the enemy's guns and said: "Yes if I could do that, I would walk straight across the valley and put my breast to one of the cannon and myself pull the lanyard."

Let me anticipate a moment that that same day, in the heat of the battle, Bliss, fighting gallantly with his regiment, was mortally wounded. The next day, I saw the Reverend Mr. Flynn, chaplain of the Eighth Georgia, who told me that Lieutenant Bliss was brought back to a farm house where a temporary field hospital had been established. He was placed on a cot and the surgeons gave him an opiate. Just before the next morning, he awoke out of his sleep, and Mr. Flynn, standing by the bed, Bliss apprehending fully where he was, spoke of his desperate wound and approaching death. Lying on his side, he asked Mr. Flynn which way was the battlefield. Mr. Flynn answered, and pointed across his body to give the true direction. Bliss said, "Won't you turn me over?" They did as he requested and then he calmly said, "I did not wish to die with my back towards the field of battle."[9]

* * *

To return to our line on Seminary Ridge, it was not long before the conference around General Lee was broken up and the different generals rode to their respective commands. In a little while our division moved to the right, and entering the skirt of woods diagonally in our rear, our movements were concealed from the enemy. We marched some two or two and one-half-miles, then halted and faced to the front. In the meantime the artillery of Longstreet's Corps was taking position, one battery after another, in the edge of the timber on the crest of the ridge. Among them was the Troup Artillery, which as well as I could judge, was the extreme right hand battery of Longstreet's guns, and its position was just a little short of fronting Round Top. We marched along in the rear of this long line of guns, the batteries being placed at intervals

The Troup Artillery position along Seminary Ridge. Jackson Giles was mortally wounded nearby.

so that the total length of Longstreet's front was probably two miles. As we passed the last of the guns, the left of Hood's Division rested upon, and supported, or was behind the Troup Artillery. The Troup Artillery was a battery from Athens, Georgia, commanded by Captain H. H. Carlton, and in it were very many boys with whom I had gone to school, or with whom their families I was well acquainted. Among these were my kinsman, Private Anderson W. Reese, and Corporal W. A. Hemphill. Beside Captain Carlton and Lieutenant C. W. Motes, there were other men of the highest grade of efficiency, which made that battery one of the best in Lee's Army.[10]

It was at this point that Hood's Division was halted and faced to the front, forming a line of battle just in the edge of the timber and concealed from the enemy. Here a delay of something like an hour occurred. General Longstreet, years afterwards, when at dinner at my house, told me that he discovered at this time that the enemy's flank to the left of Round Top was exposed. He took the responsibility of writing General Lee a note, asking permission to move his command around Round Top and attack in its rear, where the scouts had reported that the enemy's ordinance and other trains were parked. General Longstreet said, however, that the reply came: "Make the attack as ordered."[11]

A view from Seminary Ridge looking toward the Union line from the position of Anderson's Brigade.

It was whilst lying on the ground in this position, and during this delay, that we lost our first man in the battle. A shot, evidently fired at the Troup Artillery from the enemy's batteries beyond the historic peach orchard, passed across the left flank of my company. One of my men, the genial and bright young Jackson B. Giles, had been detailed as courier for General Anderson. He was a boy who had been at school with me in Monroe, Georgia, from the time he had learned his A B C's. Always cheerful, bright and willing, he was a favorite with us all. He had at this moment ridden down to our line, and just as he passed around our left flank, had dismounted from his horse with the apparent intention of lying down amongst us. Just then the shell I have mentioned tore away his left leg above the knee and dashed him ten or fifteen feet down the hill. I got up and ran to him and instantly saw, by the pallor of his face and the physical shock he had suffered, he being a rather delicate youth anyway, that he would not survive the injury. I placed him in as easy a position as possible, and told him that as soon as the litter corps came, to tell them I said carry him back to a hospital. Then I added: "Jack, you know we are going to make a charge in a few minutes, but if I ever get back to see your father and mother what message do you want me to send them?" A distinct animation came into his face as he looked straight at me and said, "Tell them I died for my country."

It is interesting to talk about the privates and line officers. We all admire the generals and our eyes kindle and beam, and our ears are full of enthusiasm as we pay deserved tributes to their fame. But it is to the private soldier and the line officers, many of them just as brave as the most famous general, to whom full justice has not been, and can never be done. And it is to me still more interesting to speak of those whom I knew in childhood and boyhood and in the peaceful walks of life, in the town and neighborhood where we lived and grew up together, and when, indulging in our boyish sports, it was never realized or even dreamed that we were to be actors together in tragedies like these. I learned afterwards that young Giles died at the hospital that same night.[12]

* * *

We soon heard the rebel yell to our right, and we knew it was General Benning and his gallant brigade, and that the charge had commenced. Instantly, the voice of General Anderson rang out like a bugle, and our brigade moved forward on the run, but with a perfect line that came of long practice, and which none but veterans could preserve under the fire we encountered as we passed through an open wheat field and across the intervening space to the enemy's position.[13]

General George T. Anderson. (GNMP)

A little way out in the field there was a staked and ridered fence. Just as I came to it I noticed John Stephens, one of our men, with his arms hanging over the topmost rail. He was a plain farmer boy who lived near my home in Walton. I had often seen him ploughing in the field, and knew him for an honest, faithful and true-hearted youth. The bullet had gone through his clothes, and I had not noticed any wound. I said, "What's the matter John?" He didn't tell me he was wounded, or complain of his hurt, but he replied: "Captain, if you will help me over the fence, I will try to go on." When he said this I got a view of his face and there, too, was the handwriting of a mortal stroke. I told him to lie down where he was and have the litter corps carry him to the rear. That night, I remembered about Stephens, and went back there before I lay down, to see in person what had been done for him. I found a new made grave. He died just where he was when the fatal bullet struck him, and where his fine spirit had still impelled him to say, "I will try to go on."[14]

Soon we encountered the enemy's main line, and in our impetuous advance we broke through them, losing quite heavily ourselves at every step, but the enemy was losing more heavily than we did, in killed, wounded and captured. This charge was made at the beginning by Hood's Division alone, and we penetrated the enemy's position a distance of three or four hundred yards. General Lafayette McLaws's Division should have charged on our left simultaneously with us, but for

The 9th Georgia advanced across this landscape. Private John Stephens was mortally wounded somewhere within this view.

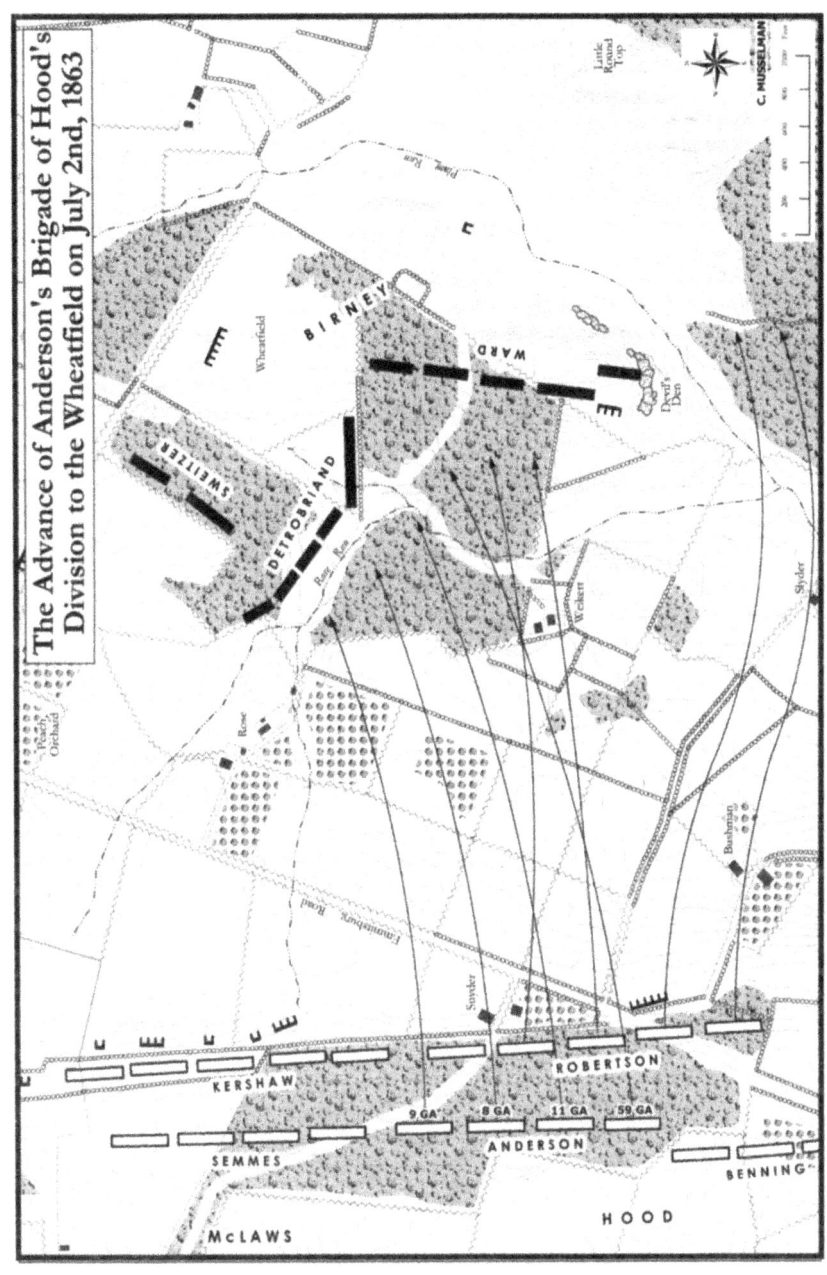

The Advance of Anderson's Brigade of Hood's Division to the Wheatfield on July 2nd, 1863

C. HUSSELMAN

Little Round Top

BIRNEY

WARD

Devil's Den

Wheatfield

SWEITZER

DETROBRIAND

Rose Run

Peach Orchard

Rose

Pickett

Snyder

Emmitsburg Road

Bushman

KERSHAW

ROBERTSON

SEMMES

9 GA   8 GA   11 GA   59 GA

ANDERSON

BENNING

McLAWS

HOOD

Sawter

some reason I have never been able to understand, his advance was delayed. When we penetrated the enemy's lines in the manner stated, our left flank naturally became very much exposed. Anderson's Brigade occupied the left of Hood's Division. The 9th Georgia Regiment, to which we belonged, was on the left of the brigade, and our Company C was the extreme left company of the regiment. I soon discovered that the bullets were coming from our front, enfilading from our left, and also diagonally from our rear. We were, however, somewhat protected by large rocks and boulders extending along just at that place.

At this time our regimental adjutant, Lieutenant Alexander Tennille, came to me and informed me that all field and line officers above me had fallen, and that the command of the regiment devolved on me. This left Lieutenant John W. Arnold in command of the company, and he did his duty well. In the next years campaign he was promoted to major and commanded the regiment to the surrender at Appomattox. Lieutenant Tennille added that General Anderson had sent him to me with directions to change the front of the three left companies so as to face the enemy on our flank. I gave the command, "Attention three left companies," but the men could not hear my voice, so great, at the moment, was the roar of musketry and artillery. Therefore, I ran to the left of the line, and touching the men on the back, made the movement known mainly by signs, and fronted the three companies to the left and rear at right

From Rose Hill looking down toward Rose's wheatfield.
Here the left flank of the Ninth became exposed to enemy
fire, and Hillyer was placed in command of the regiment.

angles to our position. In this manner the battle continued for half an hour or so, until General McLaws's troops came up on our left. His division then swept the enemy from its front, just as we had done, and restored the line. I then reformed the three left companies into their original position among the rocks, and in line with the regiment, or what was left of it.[15]

One of our company officers was Lieutenant Daniel N. Easley, who, during the battle had on a bright new uniform. I had suggested to him to take it off and wear clothes less conspicuous, but he said it was a present from home, and he was afraid he might lose the uniform if left with the baggage, and so concluded to risk it. When I made the movement of changing front a short time previously, he, with two of our men, had in some way been overlooked and had remained behind, using one of the boulders as a little fortification. When I came back to where he was, I asked him why he had not moved to the flank with the rest of the line. He said he did not hear the order, and did not know that we had changed position until, looking around, he discovered that he was alone with the two men mentioned. One of these soldiers was Ephraim Prince and the other Warren Rogers, two of my native home youths, raised in Walton County. When I came back to Lieutenant Easley, Rogers and Prince were both dead shot in the head. After the fight, Lieutenant Easley explained to me that when they were killed, one after the other, he looked up the slope and saw how greatly he would be exposed if he undertook to retreat. Lieutenant Easley was the oldest man in our company, but he was a tower of strength, although he then had a grizzled beard and gray hair. Discovering that he was alone, he determined to make the best use of his time, so taking the gun of one of his dead companions, he had employed every moment in firing from behind that rock at the enemy in front. Between them, the two who met their deaths, and Easley afterwards, had emptied both cartridge boxes.[16]

It was about this time that I saw a richly caparisoned roan horse, distant about a hundred yards, gallop riderless out from the Yankee lines, skirting along their front, and disappear in the bushes behind them. We soon ascertained that the men we were fighting belonged to General Daniel Sickles's Corps of the Federal Army. Later I saw a description of the battle written up in the New York *Herald*. From the account given of the locality where General Sickles was shot, and the description of the horse, I formed the opinion when I read that account, and think yet, that most probably it was Sickles's horse that I saw.[17]

* * *

After McLaws's Division came up on our left, our line, thus reinforced, moved some distance to the front and down a declivity into a strip
of meadow land, where a little brook ran parallel with our position. This
little brook made a natural ditch some two or three feet deep, and in its
meanderings, and with its grassy banks, made a fine natural rifle pit. We
were quick to take advantage of the opportunity and occupied it. General McLaws's men farther to our left and up the little branch or brook,
did the same thing. I saw General Paul Semmes nobly doing his duty.
He was one of the brigade commanders in McLaws's Division, and was
standing in that branch just at that part of the line next to us, occupied
by the 10th Georgia Regiment. General Semmes was killed or mortally
wounded a few minutes later. We held this rifle pit, and whilst in it did
our most effectual fighting. We met with some losses, and the water of
the brook soon became red with blood, but the enemy in the front suffered far more than we did.[18]

We could not always see distinctly, so great was the smoke, but at
intervals the smoke would lift and we had a better view. In one of those
intervals, we could see the main line of the enemy that had been attack-

*Looking westward from the meadowland and stream, up the
declivity mentioned by Hillyer. The Ninth would have
crossed this ground coming down the hill in attacks toward
the wheatfield.*

ing us. It was so thinned out as to amount to but little, so the men of my regiment were firing diagonally to our right at a column that was attacking the 8th and 11th Georgia. Just then we noticed a fresh line of the enemy which appeared to be a reinforcement, and not to have been previously engaged in the battle. They were approaching us rapidly and directly in front of my regiment, but partly concealed by the smoke. I managed to call attention to them, and the word passed down our line to hold our fire. This new regiment of the enemy came within about forty yards. Some six feet in front of them was their color bearer, a splendid looking young fellow. We could see and distinguish his features. A color guard of four or five other men were with him. His flag was a bright new one, and he gallantly waved it over his head in front. I could not hear anything that he or others of them said, nor indeed could what we said to one another be well heard, so great was the roar of battle.

Just then this color bearer stepped back into his line, and we knew that the volley was coming. With the precision of a dress parade, that magnificent line of Federals lowered their pieces and the volley came. But we had time to duck our heads and the sheet of lead passed harmlessly over us, but I could see where the bullets cut and plowed the ground behind us. Every man of us then seemed to realize our tremendous advantage. There we were in this splendid natural rifle pit, with every gun loaded. I rose up and looked along our line, and I thought then and think yet, that that volley had passed entirely harmlessly over

General Paul J. Semmes.
Captain Hillyer said he was shot
while fighting in the streambed.

Rose Run, a tributary of Plum Run, the brook from which the 9th Georgia did its best fighting.

A view northward toward the Union positions, taken from the stream bed where the "grassy bank" gave protection to Hillyer's men. The "stony hill" is to the left, and the wheatfield to the right.

our heads, and that by it we did not lose a man. Our men rested their guns on the grass in front, and with the solid line of the enemy in easy, close range, returned the fire. It seemed that not a bullet went above their heads or below their feet. They fell right and left. There was a space below the smoke of a few inches just above the ground, and we in our rifle pit, having our eyes nearly on the level of the ground, could just see below the smoke the line of their feet. This line rapidly thinned. Our men continued to load and fire. In a few minutes the fire from the enemy slackened, and some slight motion in the air lifted the smoke, and there was not one of the enemy left standing in our front. They were not all killed and wounded of course, as some had retreated. But there was a long blue line on the ground, so close together that anyone could have walked over them as far as their front extended without touching the earth. I immediately thought of that flag, and the idea occurred to me that nothing human could have gotten away with it, and that it was lying there on the ground among the heaps of those who had fallen. Stating to those near me what I was going to do, so that they might not fire on me unawares, I ran out to the place where I last saw the flag and looked all about for it; but it was not there! The man who bore it so gallantly, or some of his companions, had evidently gotten away with it. I remember to have had the momentary reflection that I hoped the color-bearer that so won my admiration, had escaped.[19]

* * *

Shortly after this, a general charge was ordered, and we advanced about a quarter of a mile farther to the foot of Little Round Top, capturing and silencing one of General Sickles's batteries on the way. The battle flag of my regiment passed through between the guns, and I saw Jim Mead, one of Company B, lay his rifle on one of the cannon, and taking deliberate but rapid aim, fire at the cannoneers of another battery on the summit of Little Round Top. But as I said, our line arrived at the foot of this noted locality, the Round Top. It was a rocky hill and about a hundred and fifty or two hundred feet high, sloping so that a person could climb it, but with difficulty. On this crest, were fifteen or twenty Federal cannon, a line of their Zouaves just in front and down the hill towards and facing us, and back of them another line equally as strong. Their combined fire was almost resistless. Our line emerged from the stumpy brush through which we had charged and came out into a long, narrow but nearly straight opening, which skirted the foot of Little Round Top, and the elevated plateau which stretched away on our left towards

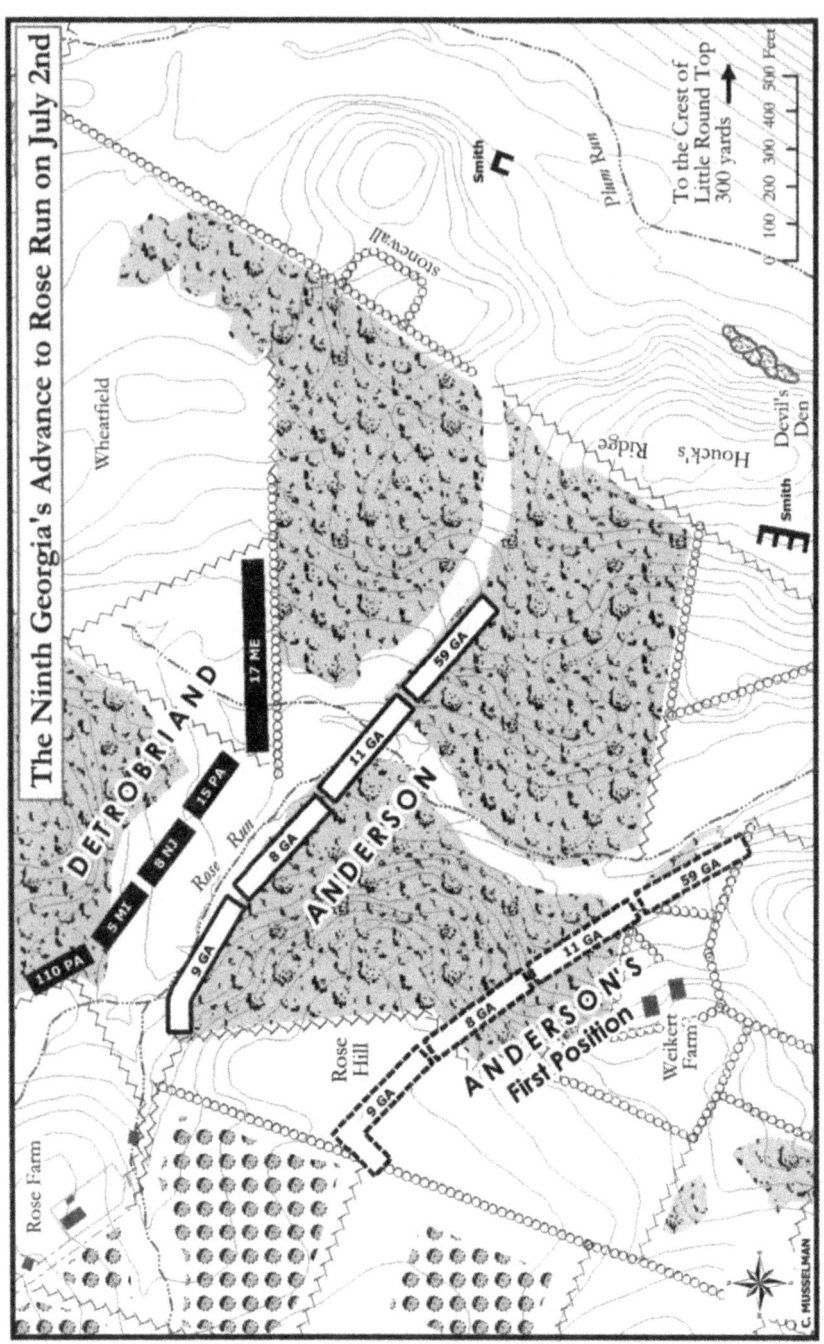

The Ninth Georgia's Advance to Rose Run on July 2nd

DE TROBRIAND

ANDERSON

ANDERSON'S First Position

Wheatfield

Rose Run

Rose Hill

Rose Farm

Houck's Ridge

Devil's Den

Weikert Farm

Smith

Smith

Smith

stonewall

Plum Run

To the Crest of Little Round Top 300 yards

0 100 200 300 400 500 Feet

110 PA
5 ME
8 NJ
15 PA
17 ME
9 GA
8 GA
11 GA
59 GA
9 GA
8 GA
11 GA
59 GA

C. MUSSELMAN

*The remnant of the battle flag of the 9th Georgia which may
have been carried through the Battle of Gettysburg.*

Georgia State Capitol Museum Collection

*Plum Run Valley and Little Round Top from the stone wall
where Hillyer and others rallied Anderson's Brigade.*

Cemetery Hill, which I mentioned awhile ago. We had then been fighting for over three hours. Although strengthened by McLaws's Division on our flank, yet neither he nor General Hood had any more than a single line, and, of course, by this time this was greatly thinned. I could see to the right and left along the opening I have mentioned, thirty-five or forty battle flags, and only from thirty to fifty men with each. On crossing this opening and going a little way up the rocky slope (by my side was Newn Hudson, now of Rockdale County), we saw that no one of the entire line was nearer to the enemy's position than we were, and that our little attacking column had hesitated. They were all veterans in the highest sense. I heard no order to retreat and gave none, but everybody, officers and men, seemed to realize that we could not carry the position, the enemy outnumbering us probably ten to one, and we exhausted, and our ranks thinned as they were. By common consent we fell back to a point where there was a stone wall. We moved back rapidly, but without panic or confusion. Just as I started back, I saw Lieutenant James Morrow, of the 11th Georgia. He said to me, "If you have been in there any further and could not do anything, there is no use for me to go." So he fell in by my side and we double-quicked back to the rock wall.[20]

I jumped on it, and by this time the firing having so far quieted that I could at least be partly heard, I called a halt. I then saw Major Henry McDaniel of the 11th Georgia do the same thing on the rock wall some fifty or seventy five yards to the right. It is my testimony that every man who heard his voice or mine, or was near enough to see and be attracted by our words and gestures, stopped at once and formed a line behind that wall. Not a man had thrown away his arms or lost his self-possession. They were as I said, veterans, and they had merely done that which best tries the mettle of the soldier, and more than all else, proves the real veteran: that is, to retreat, and if need be to retreat rapidly under fire, but without confusion and without panic. It was hardly a minute after the halt before our line was reformed, and the entire force or what was left of it, was well in hand just as much as before the charge began. From that point we moved leisurely back to the little branch or brook, the natural rifle pit I spoke of.

* * *

The enemy made no attempt to follow us or make another attack, and night soon set in. During one of the previous struggles, as the battle ebbed and flowed, there were two of the enemy who came within a few yards of our line in front of my regiment. No others got so near. In an instant one of these fell and the other dropped behind him, and once or twice loaded and fired his gun over the prostrate body of his comrade. But he too was at once killed, and when presently we advanced and passed over the ground I saw them where they lay. Afterwards, I learned that they belonged to a New York Regiment, the 101st, I think, was the number, though I am not sure as to the figures, but it was the same regiment that had fought the 9th Georgia on several former occasions. I visited the Gettysburg battlefield some six or eight years ago, and amongst the many monuments erected by the Federals, is a fine granite shaft on the spot where those men fell. It commemorates the point to which any of that command penetrated nearest to the Confederate lines. How their surviving comrades knew I cannot tell, but doubtless some were near enough to see them fall, or possibly found them there after the battle. There are, however, now many monuments on the battlefield erected by the Federals in like locales by different commands and upon the same principle. Some of them are erroneous, but this one is correct.[21]

As night came on the firing gradually ceased, and the active fighting was over for the day, though the picket firing was kept up an hour or so longer.

Soon even that also subsided, and there came an involuntary truce when the pickets of both the enemy's and Confederate lines allowed their "litter corps" to go in anywhere between the two lines to bring off the wounded. Neither side would fire on those of the other engaged in that humane duty. There were many men of our regiment lying wounded between the two lines. We expected the battle to be renewed, of course, the next morning, and we did not sleep until after one o'clock at night, when we had succeeded, according to all of the information I could get, in bringing off every one of the wounded of the regiment.[22]

It was a moonlight night, and it was whilst this humane work was going on and during the existence of the truce I have mentioned, that one of our soldiers out between the lines, I think it was one of General McLaws's men, began to sing. He was probably a boy raised in some religious home in the South, where the good old hymns were the standard music. I have heard much that the world applauds in the way of high grade music, but considering the occasion and the audience, I have never heard music like that. Many wounded from a battle can walk away, and some are carried away by the litter-bearers. But in the still air and moonlight of that night, there were hundreds, perhaps thousands of desperately wounded men lying on the ground within easy hearing of the singer, whose fine voice rang out like a flute, and echoed up and down the valley and the little mountain in our front. Not only the wounded, but also five or ten thousand and maybe more of the men of both armies could hear and distinguish the words. There was a marked silence that could come only from attention. And I think the Federal line could hear him as well as ourselves. One of the hymns he sang was this familiar one.

> Come, ye disconsolate, wherever ye languish;
> Come to the mercy seat fervently kneel,
> Hither bring your wounded hearts, here tell your anguish,
> Earth hath no sorrow that Heaven cannot heal.

The last song he sang was then familiar, but now is an almost forgotten old ditty, "When this cruel war is over." At its close, I heard a clapping of hands and a cheer from the Yankee lines. Truly, "One touch of nature makes all the world kin."

* * *

Pardon me for speaking so constantly of my own personal observations, but I could not, for want of time, go over the much disputed plan of battle, its general results and consequences. That has been well done already by many others. So by your leave, I will adhere to the thread of simply relating what I saw and heard myself, but of that only a part, a small part indeed.

We had a boy in our company named Thomas Michael. He was little more than a lad when he came to us. He was the nephew of the Michael brothers, two of our best men. They told me that Thomas had no father or mother, and was alone at home and in feeble health. On their earnest pleading, I let him remain and enlisted him, though for a long time he was not required to carry a gun, but was made useful with other duties about the camp, or on the march. Just before the beginning of the battle, Thomas happened to attract my attention. Calling him to me, I told him I wanted him to look out for a chance, and the first man who fell, get his gun and cartridge box. Then make it his business to load that gun and follow me about wherever I went, till either one or the other of us got knocked out. He was to hand me the gun and let me shoot it, then he to take and reload it, and go over the same process again. And I explained to him that I would have no time to talk, or repeat orders, but for him to keep that up no matter what happened, until the firing was over. Forty times or more in the shifting scenes of the fight, Thomas would pluck at my sleeve and hand me the gun, he holding my sword meanwhile. I would fire the gun and hand it back to him, and he kept it up to the very last. After this battle his health having greatly improved, he became a fine soldier.[23]

Between one and two o'clock at night, I lay down and slept. We had not driven the enemy as we had hoped for in the morning. Just at dusk I had heard the guns of General Ewell's Corps, which seemed to be directly in our front. I did not know that General Lee's line was in the form of a great horseshoe, and it was merely because we were on the extreme right of Lee's line that the extreme left, occupied by Ewell, seemed to be in front of us. I afterwards learned that the guns I heard were those of General Edward Johnson in the attack made by his division on Culp's Hill, on the other side of the town of Gettysburg. But I slept till daylight, when I soon learned by the picket firing that the enemy was still in force in our immediate front. This continued, without any change in position being made on either side, for hours. Hundreds of incidents collect and crowd on the mind at such a time, but of course I can only mention a few here and there.

In my regiment there were two brothers named James and William Norwood. They belonged to Captain Robert Hardee's company from Brooks County. They were very much alike, enough to have been twins. The brothers always stood or marched in the ranks side by side and were never known to be sick or off duty. Both of them were fine shots, and both usually fought on the skirmish line in front.

During the siege of Suffolk above mentioned, General Longstreet advanced our lines one foggy night, and threw up a breastwork and a fortification, into which one of our batteries was moved. The 9th Georgia Regiment was ordered up to support this battery and to occupy the line of breastworks on one side of it. When daylight came, it was discovered that a bushy cedar tree, with a trunk some six inches in thickness, was directly in the line of fire, where the artillery captain desired to direct one or more of his guns. He called down the line for a volunteer to cut down the tree. One of the Norwood brothers, the one who always carried a small axe at his belt, immediately sprang over the breastwork, and ran out to the tree about 50 yards in front and began to cut it down. After a half dozen strokes, when the trunk of the tree was about half severed, the enemy's sharpshooters opened on him a rapid and withering fire. Suddenly his grip on the axe relaxed, and his form seemed to quiver and slowly sink to the ground. In a moment the other Norwood was over the breastworks before anybody had time to caution him or stop him, and was at his brother's side. Leaning over him with his face close to his brothers, he suddenly took up the axe, and leaving his brother where he was, with a few rapid strokes quickly finished the work of felling the tree. He then turned and went rapidly back to the breastwork, sprang over it, and resumed his place without a scratch. He explained that when he went to his brother, and finding him dead, and saw there was nothing he could do for him, he thought that as he was already so much exposed, he would cut that tree down, even if it cost him his life in the attempt.

It was during the skirmish and picket fighting on the morning I last mentioned, that is, the morning of the 3rd of July at Gettysburg, that this surviving Norwood, James, was on the fighting or picket line. Since the Suffolk action he had never shown any passion or revenge, and was never heard to utter any threats. After his brother's death he continued to be the same faithful and well-liked soldier that both of them had been before, acting as if he thought it required double duty on his part, and that he must do the duty of both. Across from our picket line there was a Federal sharpshooter hidden behind a clay root,† whose fire was very accurate and very galling, and several men on our side had been pitted against him without success. James Norwood was told of it. He sent two of his companions some distance to the left, instructing them to conceal themselves and fire at that clay root continuously and as rapidly as they could, whether they saw the man behind it or not. James, in the meantime, moved a little in the other direction, so as to attack the clay root from a different angle. His instructions were followed, and the two soon had the attention of the man at the clay root centered on themselves. Meantime the Yank exposed himself a little to the unerring aim of Norwood. Soon the Yankee's gun was seen to fly up, he dropped out of sight, and there was no further annoyance from that quarter.

About six weeks after the battle, and during the time before and subsequently, Norwood was the same quiet, reliable, successful brother in every crisis. When our army had resumed its position back in Virginia near Culpepper Court House, there was a great and general inspection of General Lee's Army. General Longstreet visited, in person, I think, every regiment in his corps. I was still in command of the regiment, and he visited mine. We were drawn up for inspection in column of companies, and I walked with General Longstreet along the front of each company. Captain Hardee's Company H, that to which Norwood belonged, was one of the last that General Longstreet passed that day. He

---

† A clay root is the ball of earth and tangled roots of a tree forced above ground when a tree is blown down in a storm.

had examined many thousands of soldiers, but when he reached Norwood, whom, of course, he had never seen before, Longstreet directed the quiet, unpretending soldier to step to the front. The general took from him his gun, and with the corner of his handkerchief examined its muzzle. He then examined Norwood's uniform and his cartridge box, then handed his gun back to him, directing him to his place in the ranks. Then turning to me, General Longstreet said: "Captain, I have inspected thousands of men today and have seen nowhere a finer specimen of a soldier than this." What a fine military instinct which enabled Longstreet to judge a man with such unerring clearness, and to bestow praise where it was so well deserved.[24]

* * *

But to return to the 3rd of July. About 9 o'clock in the morning, the 11th Georgia under Major McDaniel, was withdrawn from the front line and sent to the right and rear a distance of probably a mile, to meet an attack of General H. Judson Kilpatrick's Union cavalry which were feeling our flank. As the Eleventh moved out from the timber we were in, and came in view of the enemy's cannon on Little Round Top, the cannon opened fire on them and two or three were wounded, but the regiment made the movement with entire success. Not long afterwards, an order came for the 9th Georgia to follow in the same movement. However, before moving the men, I went out on foot along where the 11th Georgia had marched. I discovered that by changing the direction, I could use the taller part of the timber as a curtain concealing my column. By this means I led the regiment from the front line back to the main body of timber in our rear on the ridge, without being seen by the enemy's batteries.[25]

On arriving at the point where the attack was being made by Kilpatrick's cavalry, I found the 7th Georgia already in position, with the 1st Texas on their left, and the 11th Georgia on their right. Just as we came up and got in touch with the actual fighting, Lieutenant Charles Maddox of the Seventh came out with his hands all bloody. He said to me that the wound he had received was such as would require him to leave the field, and that Captain William Hudson was in command of his regiment. I met Captain Hudson, and learning that his commission was junior to mine, it threw me in command of both units. I directed him to hold his position and I would support him. Soon afterwards I saw a column of Kilpatrick's cavalry break through the thin line of the 1st Texas, (the latter not having men enough to have more than about

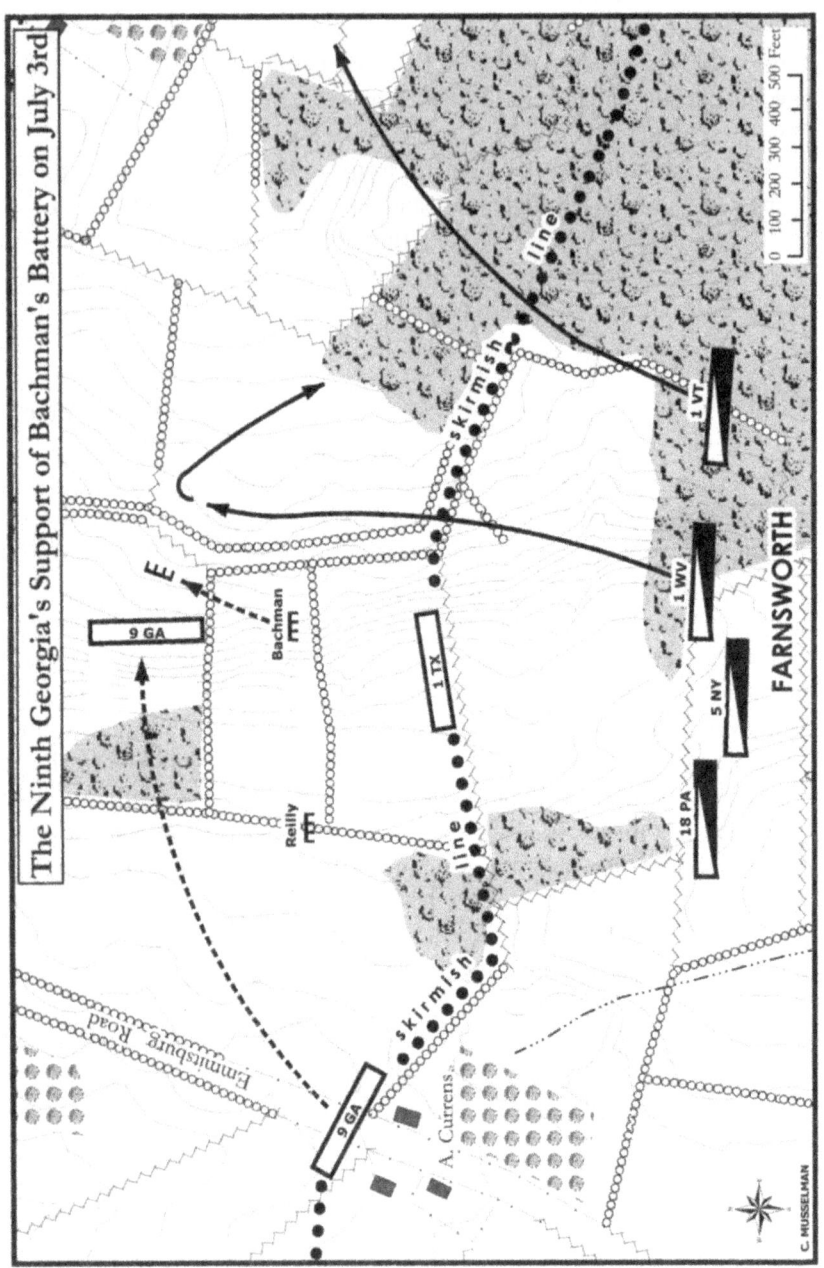

The Ninth Georgia's Support of Bachman's Battery on July 3rd

FARNSWORTH

1 VT.

1 WV

5 NY

18 PA

1 TX

9 GA

Bachman

Reilly

9 GA

Emmitsburg Road

A. Currens.

C. HUSSELMAN

0 100 200 300 400 500 Feet

skirmish line

skirmish line

one to every five or six steps). They came galloping through the intervening ground toward where one of our batteries was posted on the rising ground, to the left of where we were. I called out to Captain Hudson that the 9th Georgia was going to the support of that battery, and for him to hold his line where he was. There were some fences and other obstacles that impeded the movement of this cavalry column, who were concealed from the battery, but not from us, by a depression in the ground. They seemed in some hesitation as to which way to go, or how to make their attack, while my regiment had the advantage of open and smooth ground most of the way. So it was we succeeded in getting in behind the battery, known as Bachman's South Carolina Battery, and then advancing with my lines extended on both sides of the battery, Lieutenant Arnold cheering and leading the way. The regimental colors then came up from behind and passed between the guns, and then as we emerged from the bushes, not more than 80 yards in front of us, was this column of cavalry just on the point of making their dash at the guns.

When they saw our battle flag, they seemed to hesitate, as if they did not expect to find any infantry at that point. And, as one knows, it was rarely ever a healthy thing for cavalry to fight Confederate infantry. So it was, there was this mass of men and horses right in front of us, and in easy range. I gave the command to fire, and the volley which followed, resembled in effectiveness that of the evening before, when we were in the ditch or branch, in the main battle. The enemy's column seemed to partly go down, and what remained scattered right and left, and those who still kept on horseback, scampered into a skirt of timber some 200 yards away. One of their horses, a good bay, with black mane and tail, a Vermont Morgan horse, by some strange freak, entirely unhurt, broke away from them and galloped toward us, probably attracted by the artillery horses tethered near. I ran out and caught this horse, and being only a captain in the line (but commanding a regiment), of course I needed a mount, and this horse came in quite handy. And I will remark here, that the officers in the regiment above me, those who were not killed, were so badly wounded that it was three months before any of them returned. During that time I continued in command of the regiment, and made good use of that horse, until I turned him over to Captain Robert Holliday, Regimental Quartermaster. What was left of the attacking column of Union cavalry encountered one of General Law's Alabama regiments, which finished their discomfiture. It was then that their commander, the gallant Colonel Elon Farnsworth was killed. What few of them were left after meeting the 4th Alabama, I think it was, came

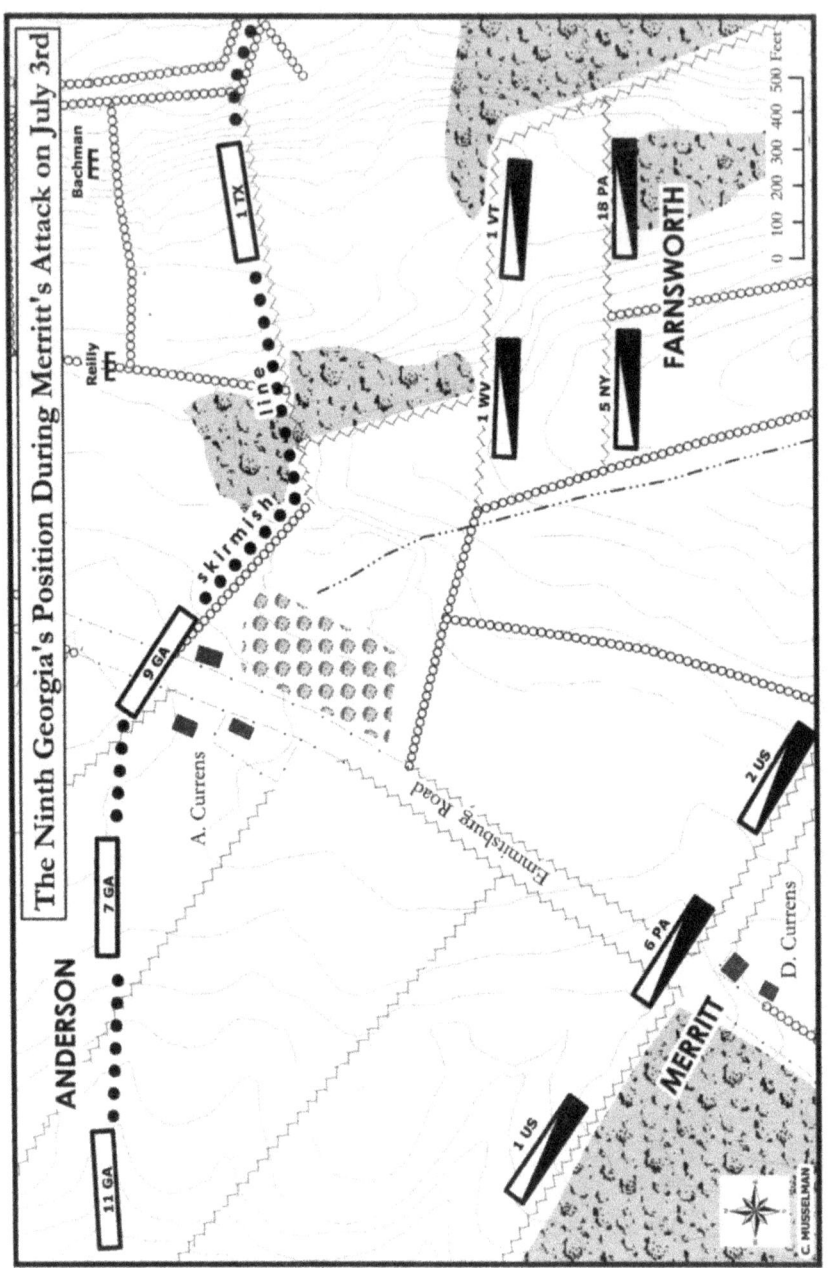

The Ninth Georgia's Position During Merritt's Attack on July 3rd

ANDERSON

11 GA
7 GA
9 GA

A. Currens

skirmish line

Bachman
Reilly

1 TX

1 VT
1 WV
5 NY
18 PA

FARNSWORTH

Emmitsburg Road

D. Currens

2 US
6 PA
1 US

MERRITT

C. MUSSELMAN

0 100 200 300 400 500 Feet

From Bachman's Battery looking over the area of the July 3 cavalry action. The stone wall occupied by the 1st Texas is down the ridge and near the woods.

out again from the woods and again encountered the fire of my regiment, and of the 1st Texas, we having them between us. And they were all killed, wounded or captured, except one within my own sight and observation, and this one man went around to the right and rear and behind the 7th Georgia, and, as I afterwards learned from them, was finally caught before he got around their line. Meantime a combined attack made by General Kilpatrick on the 7th and 11th Georgia regiments under Major McDaniel was completely repulsed by them. I think it probable that the discomfiture of this forced reconnaissance and cavalry attack was what prevented a general attack from being made by the enemy on that flank.[26]

After this combat with the cavalry, I moved the regiment to the position that had been occupied by the thin line of the 1st Texas. There, taking advantage of a rock wall, we held the position for several hours expecting to be again attacked, but the enemy did not come. The picket fighting was still going on in front all along the line. This rock wall was on the hillside, sloping toward the west. It was July and the sun was intensely hot. In front of us was a wounded Yankee cavalryman. He was crying piteously for water, and we wanted to relieve him if we could, but it was as such as any man's life was worth to expose himself in front of that wall. You might put up your hat, and a bullet would strike it in less than a minute. Littleton Rains and Robert Upshaw, two of my men, were of the litter corps and had come up and lay down with us behind the rock wall. Their litter was bloody, but just enough white shown to make it barely possible that it might be used as a flag of truce. So I told Rains to try to bring in that wounded Federal, and to wave a flag over the wall. But nobody had a handkerchief, or at least one that was white, not even as white as the cloth of the litter. So I told Rains to hold his litter up over the wall and wave it back and forth. He did so, and in two or three minutes the firing from the enemy's sharpshooters slackened and finally ceased altogether. I then told Rains to get up on the wall and wave his litter, as if for a signal, and some of the enemy stepped out in open view. Not a shot was fired at him or at them. Upshaw, the other litter bearer, then joined Rains and they got over the wall and went to where the wounded Yankee was, and brought him in and laid him down behind the wall where we gave him water, and what comfort we could. This scene was probably witnessed by hundreds of Federals, and any of them might have picked off Rains or Upshaw whilst in the act, or our men might have shot some of them, but not a gun was fired. As soon as the incident was over, however, the Federal sharpshooters, seeming to know and understand exactly what it was, and the reason it had ended, broke out again in the most business-like way and the fight went on as before. These truces to which I have alluded, were by no means exceptional, but in army experience they occurred often, and such a thing as cowardly treachery under like circumstances, or a mean shot fired taking advantage of the situation was almost or quite, unknown. Such things could not happen but for the fact that the voice of humanity in Anglo-Saxon hearts triumphed over their temptations. Doubtless the rank and file of the Federal army were better in their home and fireside teachings, and in the humanity developed in their childhood, than some of their generals.[27]

But to return to the rock wall. After awhile Major William Sellars of General Hood's staff (though Hood had before that been badly wounded, and General Law was commanding), brought me an order to move my regiment to its original position supporting the 7th Georgia. At the same time he complimented us for the good work we had done in repulsing the enemy's cavalry column. It was during these operations, when my regiment was fighting the cavalry, that Pickett's charge was made some two miles to the left of us, on the center of the enemy's position. The intervening wood prevented us from seeing what occurred in that charge, even if the severe work we were doing ourselves had not fastened our attention and kept us busy. We heard the cannonading, and the combined roar of nearly 300 guns that had made the ground tremble.

I would not pluck one laurel from General George Pickett or his men, or from their memory. Nevertheless it is a fact, that in our two days' fighting at Gettysburg, both the 8th and 9th Georgia lost a larger percentage of men actually killed and wounded than did any regiment in Pickett's command. And this was equally true of the 11th Georgia.

We spent the night after the third day's battle on the line where we had encountered the cavalry, that line being held by the 1st Texas, and the 7th, 9th and 11th Georgia regiments. There was little or no fighting during the 4th of July, and the next morning General Lee withdrew his army from the field. We marched leisurely over the same ridge of mountains I mentioned at the start, but crossing a gap further to the south, our column emerged at Hagerstown, Maryland. Here we halted a few days, and it was whilst we were here encamped on the banks of the Antietam, some miles above the old Antietam, or Sharpsburg battlefield, that I wrote my report of the Gettysburg battle.[28]

What follows is the official report of the battle Captain Hillyer wrote for his superiors.

Camp near Hagerstown, Md.,
July 8, 1863.

Captain:

I have the honor to report that about 4 o'clock in the afternoon during the battle of Gettysburg, on the 2d instant, all officers senior to me having fallen, the command of this regiment devolved upon me, and during the remainder of the battle, both that day and the next, and until the present time, I have continued in command, and it now becomes my duty to report the part taken by the regiment in the action.

Lieutenant-Colonel John C. Mounger was killed by a piece of shell soon after the advance commenced, while leading the regiment with his characteristic gallantry, and for about an hour afterward Major William M. Jones was in command, when he and Captain James M.D. King were both wounded, and taken from the field nearly at the same moment.

The regiment occupied its usual position in line on the left of the brigade and the extreme left of the division, having for nearly an hour and a half no support on its left, the advance of McLaws' division being for some reason thus long delayed, which left the flank while advancing nearly the distance of a mile very much exposed to an enfilading fire of the enemy's batteries, and also to the fire of a flanking party of the enemy, who were prompt to take advantage of the exposed condition of the flank. To meet this flanking party, I changed the front of three companies, and for nearly an hour, against great odds, held them in check until relieved by the advance of McLaws' division, which finally came up on our left.

The whole line now again pressed forward, and, though entirely without support, dispersed and scattered a fresh line of the enemy who came up against us, and pursued them 400 or 500 yards farther to the base of the mountain upon which the enemy's heavy batteries were posted, which we found to be the strongest natural position I ever saw. Our little band, now thinned and exhausted by three and a half hours' constant fighting, made a gallant attempt to storm the batteries, but the enemy being again heavily re-enforced, we were met by a storm of shot and shell, against which, in our worn out condition, we could not advance. I believe that had McLaws' division advanced with our line so that we could have arrived at this point before we became worn out with fatigue, we would have carried the position.

In this movement the whole brigade and also several brigades of McLaws' division participated. Failing to take the batteries, the line retired to the point where we first encountered the enemy's main line, and was again formed, fronting the enemy in such position as to place most of the battle-field in our possession. The enemy evidently had enough of it, and did not again show himself in our front, darkness soon closing the scene.

The regiment lost 2 officers (Lieutenant-Colonel Mounger and Lieutenant E.W. Bowen) killed, and 11 officers wounded; also 25 enlisted men killed and 119 men wounded, and 1 officer and 31 men missing; total, 189.

There were many officers and men who displayed a degree of daring and heroism which challenges admiration in the very highest degree, and the whole regiment behaved with its customary steadiness and devotion, as the loss of 189 out of 340 carried into the field will testify.

I herewith respectfully submit a detailed statement of casualties, giving names and description of wounds in full, from which I have omitted all slight wounds, which, though sufficient to disable the man for a day or two, will not prevent his taking part in the next battle — say a week or ten days from the time the hurt was received. On the next day (3d instant), the regiment was detached from the brigade, and sent to drive off the enemy's cavalry, who were annoying our batteries on the extreme right flank. Here the regiment, though exhausted by the extreme heat and by long-continued exertion, performed, without a murmur, but, on the contrary, with the greatest enthusiasm, much hard marching and fighting, as the enemy's mounted men frequently changed their point of attack, which rendered a change of position on our part also often necessary. At one time two or three squadrons of their cavalry charged through the picket line of the First Texas Regiment, and were galloping up to one of our batteries, with the evident purpose of spiking the guns. This regiment [the 9th Georgia] was at the time some distance to the right of the First Texas, and at a point which was not then menaced. I therefore led the regiment to the battery at a double-quick, something more than half a mile off, and while going there received, through Major William H. Sellers, an order directing me to do so.

When we arrived, the enemy were nearly at the battery. Passing through from behind the guns, with a yell the regiment charged the enemy in the open field, scattering and chasing them away in a moment, killing and wounding a number and capturing several horses. This was the first repulse that this column met with, and their advance was first checked by this regiment. When they fled from us, they encountered several other regiments who were coming up from different points, and suffered greatly from their fire. During the first day's fight [meaning July 2], a large number of prisoners were passed to the rear through the lines of the regiment, but in the eagerness of our attack no guard was sent with them to the rear, and I cannot give the number. According to my observation, the enemy's loss was five times as great as ours.

Very respectfully, &c.,
Geo. Hillyer,
Captain, Commanding Ninth Georgia Regiment.

Capt. Charles C. Hardwick,
Assistant Adjutant-General.[29]

* * *

The following letter was written by Captain Hillyer to his father Junius Hillyer, three days after he completed the above official report of the Battle of Gettysburg. Mr. Hillyer sent it to an Athens, Georgia newspaper, the **Southern Banner,** *where it was published July 29, 1863. The article was prefaced by Junius Hillyer with these words: "Permit me to state that it was written* *hurriedly [by my son] on many scraps of paper with a pencil, under circumstances of great personal discomfort, and without any expectation of its publication.*"

July 11th, at Sundown

My Dear Father

The army is at this time encamped in line of battle stretching away from the Potomac river to and beyond Hagerstown, expecting and preparing for an attack from the enemy. Of all the circumstances of our position and situation, I must not speak; for the long line of our communications is liable to raids by the enemy's cavalry, and our mails liable to capture.

Our Brigade had an encounter yesterday beyond our lines, on the other side of Antietam river, where we were sent by Gen. Stuart, where we lost 200 men killed and wounded. My Regiment, the 9th, lost some of its best men killed and two excellent officers wounded. The regiment behaved as steadily as on dress parade. The 59th, from some cause, fell back, which exposed the flank of the 11th, and in succession of the 7th, 8th, and finally of the 9th, when I was compelled to give the order to retire, which was slowly and sullenly obeyed. It was reported — I do not know the fact — that the reason the 59th fell back, was that our artillery, by some mis-management was firing into them. In my company Rains was wounded, (a flesh wound in the shoulder,) and Jasper McGaughey lost his left leg below the knee. Capt. Scott, Lieutenants Arnold, Early, and Morrow, and Anderson Reese are up to this time safe. — I am informed that our cousin, Lieutenant Hillyer, of the 3rd Georgia is also unhurt. — Major McDaniel was seriously wounded in the abdomen — I fear mortally. He bore himself manfully in all the battles and endures his sufferings like a hero. He was left in comfortable quarters at a private house in Funkstown, and will, I fear, fall into the hands of the enemy.

July 12th. — I wrote the above yesterday morning, sitting by a tree at the Surgeon's quarters, where I had gone weary and exhausted, to get a little medicine — having some fever — and to try and get some rest, which I greatly need. I was interrupted by an order for the Hospital to be moved to the place selected by the Division surgeon, in anticipation of the coming battle. I got in one of the ambulances and rode out to the place selected, turning over for the time, the command of the regiment to Captain Webb. It is now noon, and there are no signs of the enemy in our front. Our men are busily engaged throwing up entrenchments on the line about a mile off, in view of where I now sit writing. I hope to be well enough to go back to the battle tomorrow. I have no fear or dread when in the line of my duty.

The enemy seem reluctant to attack us here, and it may be that he does not intend doing so at all — knowing that the want of subsistence will soon compel Lee to cross the river. The enemy suffered more at Gettysburg than we did, and although we failed to drive him from the Gibraltar he had chosen on the mountains, yet our infantry did all along the line get access to his, and his losses were greater than ours. The truth is, the battle was like Sharpsburg and Murfreesboro in its results, though far more extensive and sanguinary than either.

Our position here is comparatively an open country, and if Meade attacks us the chances are very great that we will destroy his army. The fight which my regiment had with the enemy's cavalry at the battle of Gettysburg, (about which I wrote you in a former letter,) has given us much eclat in all our part of the army. We charged upon and dispersed double our number of cavalry in an open field and chased them around its fences and adjacent woods, killing and wounding a great many. While flying from my regiment, they ran into the fire of several other regiments and became so entangled that but few escaped.

I should be rejoiced more than I can possibly express, if I could see you to talk of my regiment and brigade and division, and of the fate and deeds of my brave comrades and of my own adventures. To write it, would be, situated as I am, impossible. At the battle of Gettysburg, where Longstreet's corps was engaged on the 2d, our division, (Hood's) began the attack, and for near two hours sustained the shock of battle alone. After we had penetrated several hundred yards into the enemy's lines, our flanks were, of course, very much exposed. My regiment is the extreme left of the division, and my company the extreme left of the Regiment, so that the position of my company was the worst of all. For nearly an hour the enemy were on three sides of us, and a battery of sixteen guns enfilading us with grape. If it had not been for the shelter of rocks and trees behind which we fought, not one of us would have escaped. I changed the front of the three left companies so as to face the enemy every way, and we held the enemy at bay until the flank was relieved by the coming up of McLaws' division. By this time our division had whipped and dispersed two lines of the enemy, which they had successively encountered, and just about the time McLaws came up, the enemy strongly reinforced his whole line. But half an hour's hard fighting caused them to retreat again. It was now nearly sundown. But simultaneously from all along our line, there went up a yell only such as our army can give when rushing on the foe. True, we were wearied and exhausted, and our ranks were thinned by the long contest, but we went forward as fast as we could through the rocky woods in which we had been fighting, across the disputed valley, up the hill beyond, (the enemy all the while falling and flying before us for more than half a mile), when we came to a long open ravine, beyond which rose a steep rocky ridge, some hundred and fifty feet high, everywhere crowned with Artillery. I saw the cannon belching forth volumes of smoke all along the summit, but heard no report from them — the roar of musketry and the shouts of our men drowned every other sound. We did not pause or hesitate a moment, but advanced after emerging from the timber one or two hundred yards, to the very foot of the hills and within a stone's throw of the cannon. During this charge, I saw our men falling in large numbers, and the enemy's infantry who were retreating before us, suffered very heavily, particularly as they went up the hill. I saw the ground ploughed and torn by grapeshot and shell — still I heard no distinct sound, so great was the roar and din of battle. If we had been fresh, we would have taken the hill, but when we got to the foot of it and saw how steep it was, and how high it was, and how much our ranks were thinned, all seemed at once to perceive that the desperate effort must fail, and we turned and retired to a selected line in the woods. Do not think me vain. I will say that I am proud of my regiment, and of my division, and I am proud of my company, and of all these I am justly proud. I am sorry we could not take the hill, but I have no self-accusation for the failure, for I went as near the enemy's guns as any other man, and at the foot of the hill fired my rifle at the cannoniers. When we dressed our line in the woods, and prepared to renew the conflict, I had scarcely eighty men left in the regiment and it was found that 244 out of 310 had been disabled. I had command of the regiment by the fall of senior officers since about the time McLaws' Division joined us. Thus ended the battle for that day. The next day, in the battle of Friday, we were detached and fought the enemy's cavalry. In a letter like this, I must omit many incidents, of which I would like to speak. And I have referred only to the movements of Longstreet's corps, and particularly of Hood's Division — of what transpired around me and what I saw. Of the position and events in front of Ewell and A.P. Hill, I know little more than you do. For the satisfaction of friends at home I will add that we brought off and decently buried every man that was killed in the regiment. Our wounded, except the few who were too badly hurt to be moved, we had brought off and cared for. Poor Jack Giles (I know how much you respected and esteemed his father) had his leg torn off by a shell just before we began to advance. He was about ten steps from me at the time, I went to him, and at once saw by his countenance and his extreme prostration that he would die. I asked him what I must tell his father and his mother, in case I should live to see them. Shells were tearing the trees and the ground around us, but the heroism of his spirit triumphed even in that dreadful hour. His reply was simple and calm — "Capt. tell my father and my mother I died for my country." May God rest his soul, and temper this second great grief for his aged parents. He was the only one of our boys who were killed, that I saw before death after they were struck. All the rest of my company that were killed, Rogers, Atkinson and Stephens and Ragan, were good soldiers and much esteemed. My heart is deeply afflicted with sorrow when I think of them and of their far distant friends. Jasper McGauhey, who was wounded and lost his leg on the 10th, in the fight at Funkstown, was left at a hospital in Williamsport. I saw him yesterday, the 13th. He seemed to mind it very little, and I think he will do well. Ephraim Prince — wounded at Gettysburg — poor fellow, could not be moved. He was shot through both thighs, one of which was broken. Jack McDaniel was wounded across the back, injuring the spine, and he could not be moved, though his wound is not thought to be mortal. Both of these were left at the field hospital near Gettysburg, and have fallen into the hands of the enemy. Their friends will of course be anxious about them. But I have little doubt the enemy will treat them kindly. We left ample nurses, supplies, and physicians with them. Bill Brown and John Perkins were sent out on horseback to forage for the hospital and unluckily were captured. Jim Conner and Wilson Woodruff are also thought to be prisoners, as they are missing. Our other wounded — a list of whom has been published — were at last accounts doing well. They have all been sent forward to Staunton and Winchester. I heard from Major McDaniel three days after he was wounded, when he was better and hoped to do well.

I wonder somebody don't take to puffing the 9th regiment. It is one of the best and steadiest on the continent. But no pains having been taken to noise it in the newspapers, I suppose people at home know very little about it.

Affectionately, your son,
George Hillyer.[30]

* * *

The Battle of Gettysburg was certainly the high point in the military career of Captain George Hillyer, and within a few months of that engagement, his life took on a whole new direction. Even as early as the end of July, Hillyer felt his association with the 9th Georgia was coming to an end. Because the Ninth elected its officers, the captain, then still in temporary command realized he would never attain higher rank. He explained why in a July 28 letter to Richmond authorities, when he sought permission to organize a cavalry regiment in order to secure a colonel's commission. In that correspondence, Hillyer wrote: "My efforts in the enforcement of discipline has not increased the number of those disposed to put [me] in permanent command." The request for transfer to enlist a new regiment was quickly approved by General Evander Law (commanding Hood's Division), who called Hillyer "an officer of intelligence and energy." Unfortunately, Generals Longstreet and Lee overruled Law, probably because they needed their best men to remain with the Virginia army. Eventually, all of this wrangling came to nothing. For in the fall of the year, on October 17, 1863, Captain Hillyer escaped the opportunity for promotion, or even the chance of death on the battlefield, when he tendered his resignation from Confederate service. The reason for his resignation came about as a result of a request made by Georgia's Governor Joseph E. Brown. Governor Brown needed a man with a military background to fill the office of Auditor for a state-controlled railroad named the *Western & Atlantic*. This line was important to the governor because it was the main supply transportation for General Joseph E. Johnston's Army of Tennessee. The governor said Hillyer was "a man of pure morals & unblemished character [who] has seen much military service during the war." The appointment to this significant post lasted until the end of hostilities, and one of its duties entailed the organization of a militia unit to guard the road. Therefore, soon after accepting the position, Captain Hillyer enlisted a battalion of railroad men, and was placed in command with the rank of major. In 1865, with the failure of the Confederate cause, Major Hillyer surrendered himself and his men to Federal troops in Atlanta. He and his troops were paroled, and all returned to civilian life.

As a soldier no longer, ex-captain Hillyer had to determine a way to make a living in a Southland that was changed forever. Fortunately for this 30 year old Georgian, his options were many, unlike what most other army veterans faced in those confused times of upheaval, and hardship. George Hillyer was by all accounts, better prepared to enter the work force of a defeated country still in shambles after four years of bloody and destructive war. He had been born into a hard working, successful family with a long heritage on American soil. One of his ancestors was John Hillyer who had settled in New England in 1639. George's own grandfather, Shaler Hillyer, moved to Georgia around the year 1800. George Hillyer's parents, Jane Selina Watkins and Junius Hillyer, were themselves well educated and comfortably situated when George was born in Athens, Clarke County, Georgia, on March 17, 1835. (According to family history, George had hazel eyes, and was later described as being short in stature, but with a strong intellect, and a forceful personality). Junius Hillyer would have been an excellent role model for any young man. Both of his grandfathers had served in the Revolutionary War, and he held a law degree that had been earned at the University of Georgia in 1828. By 1851, when George was sixteen, the elder Hillyer had already served as a judge on the superior court, and had just been elected to the United States Congress. George Hillyer's first real schooling took place at a local academy in Walton County, a few miles southwest of Athens, where the family was then living. In 1854 George graduated with honors from Penfield College (now Mercer University, Macon), and went immediately to work for his father's law practice. Shortly thereafter, in 1855, he was admitted to the bar, and in 1857 received his Master of Arts degree. During the years from 1857 to the commencement of the war in 1861, George Hillyer practiced law in partnership with his father and later with an attorney named Hope Hull. Between 1857 and 1858, he was elected to and served in the Georgia House of Representatives. From 1859 to 1860 he held the title of Chief Clerk in the same legislative body, and in the latter year he was one of the delegates to the Democratic National Convention in Charleston.

There is a good possibility that George Hillyer could feel change coming during his tenure at the Charleston convention. And while we do not know positively how he felt about secession, he did voice these sentiments to a group of Confederate veterans in 1904: "Comrades, we broke no law and committed no crime. We fought in a just cause; we were right then and we are right now…. We lifted our hands in our own defense." So there can be no surprise that when the opening guns spoke loud and clear over Fort Sumter on April 12, George Hillyer had already taken action toward his beliefs. Just prior to the commencement of the war he had organized and assumed command of a volunteer cavalry company in Walton County, Georgia. This force was dismounted two months later, in June 1861, because the governor of Georgia would not accept any more mounted units into state service. The men then "took the musket" Hillyer said, and converted to foot soldiers, becoming the "Hillyer Rifles." The "Rifles" soon mustered into the Confederate army as Company C, 9th Regiment, Georgia Infantry. As captain, Hillyer, his servant Alex (who remained a lifelong and trusted companion), and his men shared the hardships of active field service for twenty-eight months. This long period of soldiering, during the various seasons of the year, included much tedious camp life, exhausting, long and dirty marches, and campaigns filled with tiny skirmishes and large crushing battles. And, always hovering nearby, stood grim death, in the guise of lingering disease or mortal wounds. Through it all Captain Hillyer stood side by side with his lieutenants, sergeants and privates. Before the war he was a prosperous and privileged man, but in 1861 he became just another infantryman trying to stay clean and alive. From the Yorktown Siege in April 1862, through combat at Williamsburg, Mechanicsburg, and then the Seven Days Battles, Garnett's and Golding's Farms, and Malvern Hill, he led his little company through the war-ravaged Virginia countryside. Then there were still more battles at Rappahannock Station, Thoroughfare Gap, Second Manassas, Sharpsburg, Fredericksburg (where he first commanded the regiment), Suffolk, Gettysburg, and Funkstown. And finally the end came for Hillyer after the Chickamauga Campaign, in his own home state of Georgia. Parting from his comrades in the old Ninth Regiment must have been bittersweet. However who could blame the captain, if, by seeking higher office, he also escaped the brutal realities of total war. But Hillyer also had no reason to feel ashamed of his military record. General Hood knew that to be true, when he called Hillyer "a most able, efficient, & gallant officer," and said that the captain was "competent to command a Regiment, [and] but few Regiments in the Service will be under better discipline than the one he is honored with the command of."

Upon Hillyer's return to civilian life in 1865, his first decision was to relocate to Atlanta, where he attempted to sort out the confused affairs of the state's railroads. In 1867, on June 25, he married Ellen Emily Cooley of Rome, Georgia. They eventually had seven children: Elisabeth, Mary (Minnie), Marian, George, Jr., Ellen, and three who did not survive infancy, Daisy, Hollis, and Emily. During the post-war years George Hillyer continued his law practice, but seemed always drawn to the excitement and challenge of politics. Some of his many achievements in this civic arena are worth mentioning. In 1869 Hillyer was again made Auditor for the *Western & Atlantic*. From 1871-1874 he served in the Georgia Senate from the 35th District. During 1873-1876 he held the post of Centennial Commissioner for the State of Georgia. Between 1877-1883 he was judge of the state circuit court for the Atlanta district. Furthermore, between 1885-1886 Hillyer officiated as mayor of Atlanta, and both in 1884 and 1892 was again chosen as a delegate to the Democratic National Convention. In 1899 Judge Hillyer retired from the active practice of law, yet in 1907 he was appointed to the state railroad commission. It was expressed by his peers at the time, that Judge Hillyer could have readily been elected to the United States Congress, however Ellen flatly refused to move to Washington, so the question was put to rest. Other contributions made to the community included membership on Atlanta's Board of Water Commissioners, (for 12 years), where he made "a close study of the water systems of several cities and was the author of articles upon the subject in many technical journals." George Hillyer was also a steadfast friend to the black population of Georgia, and during his lifetime made great efforts to see that the newly freed slaves were given their rights and benefits under state and federal laws. He always blamed the U. S. government for abandoning the Negroes after the war, and during the turbulent reconstruction years. Helping the poor and educating the young, for both blacks and whites, were two of his favorite causes. He was for many years, a member of the Southern Baptist Home Mission Board, and was a trustee for Mercer University, Atlanta Medical College, Atlanta College of Physicians and Surgeons, Spelman Seminary, and Atlanta University, the last two being black institutions. And, as a long-standing member of the Baptist Church, Judge Hillyer was often chosen as a delegate to the periodic conventions of that denomination.

While George Hillyer certainly led an intensive and colorful schedule in the years between the war and his death, one activity always claimed the affection of his heart, and was accorded much respect, time, and energy. This area was, of course, the concern and friendship he felt for his old comrades-in-arms. As their former captain, Hillyer never let an opportunity pass to meet with or aid one of his ex-soldiers. (He even attended the great reunion during the 50th Anniversary of the Battle of Gettysburg in 1913). Activities concerning Confederate survivors were a high priority for Judge Hillyer, and as a member of the United Confederate Veterans he was elected to and served as the Commander-General of Georgia. His warm feelings toward his men never wavered. An example comes down to us in the words he wrote to one of the past privates of Company C, who had asked Hillyer's recommendation for a veteran's commendation. Writing in 1895 to Sampson M. Sill, a twice wounded and brave member of the Ninth, Hillyer said: "This is a labor of love and I would not have a cent for it. I would rather get up at midnight or walk 25 miles to do you a kindness than to charge you anything for this service…. The honorable record you made, you may safely hand down as a rich heritage to your children, and your children's children."

Considering the many dangers that Captain Hillyer survived between 1861 and 1864, it is a little remarkable how his death came about. At the age of 92, while feeding some chickens behind his house at 818 Springdale Road in Atlanta, a rooster jumped up and pecked Hillyer's ear. The ear became infected, and the infection spread to his brain, causing his death two weeks later on Sunday, October 2, 1927. It comes as no surprise that thousands of mourners attended Judge Hillyer's funeral

George Hillyer in 1919 wearing his United Confederate Veteran's uniform.

the following day, including the Governor of Georgia and the Mayor of Atlanta, as well as scores of friends, relatives, and a contingent of ex-soldiers from United Confederate Veterans Camp # 159. The rites were conducted at 2:30 p.m. in the Second Baptist Church, where Hillyer had held membership for 60 years. The old soldier was then buried in a simply ceremony in the family lot in Oakland Cemetery, "in a quiet corner ... where the calm and serenity is scarcely disturbed by the echoes of the forward march of the city whose progress he aided so materially in building."[31]

* * *

Judge Hillyer as he appeared during the final years of his life.
(Bernard W. Wolff)

In the Footsteps of Captain Hillyer

A walking tour of the battlefield traversed
by the 9th Georgia on July 2, 1863

For anyone interested in following the movements of Captain Hillyer and the 9th Georgia Regiment, we have included a tour that will lead you from Seminary Ridge to the base of Little Round Top. During this walk of approximately one hour, you will see places that the captain described in his narrative, while traversing the very ground crossed by the author in 1863.

To prepare for the tour, be sure to dress properly. Obviously, during the winter and spring the path may be snow covered, or just wet and muddy. In the summer and fall you will find generally dry conditions, but expect thick grass, and some heavy undergrowth.

Our first order of business is to get to the starting point and park. There are several choices for this step. One is simply to drive to the site, take the tour, and then walk back to your car. A second option is to have a partner drop you off on Seminary Ridge, and pick you up later on Ayers Avenue, where the tour ends. If making the trek alone, consider parking along Ayers and then walking out to Seminary Ridge. That way, when the tour is completed, you are already at your vehicle, and ready to return home.

To BEGIN THE TOUR, go to the observation tower on West Confederate Avenue. From the parking area, walk southward along the edge of the woods and the stone wall, past the South Carolina Monument to the Troup Artillery's iron marker on the right side of the road. This position was the left flank of Anderson's Georgia Brigade. It is also the area where Captain George Hillyer and the men of the 9th Georgia halted for the last time, before going into battle with Hood's Division just prior to 4 p.m. on July 2. Although Hillyer is unclear about the whereabouts of the Lieutenant Fred Bliss incident, this locale may be where the story took place. It is almost certainly the ridge on which Private Jackson Giles had his leg torn off by a Union artillery shell, and then said to Hillyer, "Tell them I died for my country." Directions to the field hospital where Bliss and Giles died will be given at the conclusion of the tour. And remember, as you walk along, take time to read excerpts from Hillyer's observations as the battle raged around him.

Now, WALK BACK ACROSS THE ROAD to the stone wall and to the tablet designating Cabell's Artillery Battalion. Stand at the wall to the left of the tablet. From here you can recognize the low ridge to the east indicating Little Round Top. (A monument is sometimes visible on the summit) Big Round Top is to the right and plainly visible. Where you stand was the extreme left of Hood's Division, which on that day stretched off to the right for about three-quarters of a mile. Here is the part of the ridge where Company C, 9th Georgia Infantry rested before the attack. As Captain Hillyer indicated, his small company of approximately 35 men occupied the far left of the entire division.

FROM THE WALL, look out across the open ground in front of you, which Hillyer said was a wheat field in 1863. About half way to the tree line is the Emmitsburg Road. Walk to the road, and stop at the large green metal utility box on the eastside of the road. (As you traverse these open spaces, please be considerate of any farm crops growing there.) Once at the box, there is a good view of George and Dorothy Rose's stone farmhouse. Ahead is Rose Hill, a little beyond the fence, and out in front of the wood line. Somewhere in this vicinity, Private John Stephens was struck down by enemy fire and died. Here too, between Seminary Ridge behind you, and Rose Hill in front, Lieutenant Colonel John Mounger and other officers and men of the Ninth were injured or killed during the initial advance of Anderson's Brigade. Most of the artillery fire that hit the Georgians came from Union guns at the "Peach Orchard" and along Wheatfield Road far out to your left.

ONCE YOU HAVE CROSSED THE NEXT FIELD, stop at the low stone wall where the wood and/or wire fence meet. The small, but distinct shape of Rose Hill can be clearly seen just in front of you. This old wall was likely where the 9th Georgia rallied after being driven back from its first advance position down over the hill and at the edge of Rose's wheatfield. To the left stands the Rose house built about 1820. George Rose's brother John was operating this 230-acre farm in 1863 and his family occupied the dwelling. The brigades of General's Kershaw and Semmes fought over the terrain to your left about an hour after Anderson's men arrived here. (For your information, one regiment of 350 soldiers, formed in two ranks from left to right, could extend for about 60 yards. Therefore Anderson's Brigade had a battlefront of approximately 300 yards.)

WALK OVER ROSE HILL to the wooden "snake or worm fence" just inside the tree line. Here amidst scattered large rocks and boulders, is where the Ninth halted for the first time to rest and reform the regimental lines after its harrowing movement across the open fields to the west. However, there was little time to take a breath, as Union artillery and musketry fire opened even more intensely on the exhausted Georgians. Several events described by Captain Hillyer occurred in this vicinity. It was here that Hillyer was notified that the command of the regiment had devolved on him. Furthermore, in this locale, General Anderson directed Hillyer to face three companies to the left in order to deflect incoming fire from an enemy flanking party. And too, this was the place where Captain Hillyer saw the runaway horse he thought belonged to General Sickles. Finally, you are probably fairly close to the large boulder used for cover by Lieutenant Easley and Privates Prince and Rogers, and where the two privates were shot.

FROM THE WORM FENCE, move forward to the monument of the 145th Pennsylvania Infantry just across Brooke Avenue. (It's the one with the soldier holding his musket out to the front). This line of Union memorials represents the position taken by Colonel John Brooke's brigade of the Second Corps, after it assisted in pushing Anderson's Brigade back from the south end of Rose's wheatfield below. From a point behind this monument (and depending on the amount of foliage in bloom), one can sometimes discern a portion of the "Wheatfield" and Rose Run, just ahead and down the hill. More importantly to our concern though, is the "declivity" mentioned by Hillyer: it is right in front of you. After being reinforced by General Kershaw's South Carolina Brigade, the captain noted: "Our line...moved...down a declivity into a strip of meadow land, where a little brook ran...."

WALK DOWN THE HILL to Rose Run, and proceed to the small bridge that spans the stream. From the bridge itself, there is a nice view back up the "declivity" just traversed. Facing front again, the clearing of Rose's famous "wheatfield" is straight ahead. In addition, the "stony hill" (mentioned in General Kershaw's battle report), is visible to the left, at the end of the path. To your front and rear flows the stream with the "grassy banks" described by Hillyer, which he said made a "fine natural rifle pit." This is where the 9th Georgia did its most effective fighting. If you wish, step down onto a dry spot in the streambed, and read Captain Hillyer's account of the combat he and his men experienced here, as the water in the brook "became red with blood."

NEXT, FOLLOW THE PATH a short distance toward the "stony hill" out to DeTrobriand Avenue. Turn right along the avenue and walk to the monument dedicated to the 110th Pennsylvania (It is surmounted by a soldier standing with a musket). Captain Hillyer recalled encountering a memorial during his visit to Gettysburg around 1897. This could have been the monument he saw. However, Hillyer mistakenly thought it was the 101st New York, and said it marked the advance position of two brave Federal soldiers who died there in 1863.

CONTINUE ALONG THE AVENUE INTO THE WHEATFIELD. In this segment of the tour, you are generally moving in the direction traveled by the Ninth in its last attack against Federal units that were falling back to Cemetery Ridge. In the final assault, Anderson's Georgians were accompanied on the left by the brigades of Generals Semmes, Kershaw, and Wofford. In your walk, observe the large leaning White Oak to the right and just off the avenue. It is one of the few remaining trees that was growing on the field in 1863, making it a true "witness" to the battle. Next, glance at the stone wall also coming up on the right side. It was along this wall that two of General Anderson's regiments (the Eight and Eleventh), battled defending Union troops late on the afternoon of July 2. As you approach the stop sign at Sickles Avenue, the last monument on your right is that of the 4th Michigan. It is possible that the regiment decimated by the Ninth from its position in the streambed was the 81st Pennsylvania. Their color bearer was described by Hillyer as "a splendid looking young fellow," who might have been James "Reddy" McHale. The monument to that unit is ahead, right out in the open field. If it is indeed the correct regiment, then you are standing near where Captain Hillyer ran to, to recover the fallen flag.

AT THE STOP SIGN, walk to the right and follow the avenue until it turns slightly and disappears into the woods. Here on the left side of the road is a black and silver painted metal plaque that reads "WHEAT-FIELD." North of this sign is the hulking monument to the 148th Pennsylvania Infantry. From the monument, go a few yards more to Ayres Avenue. Follow Ayers to the right and through the woods toward the distant outline of Little Round Top. Just beyond the wood line, in the open and parallel to the hill, is a low stone wall. At this historic little wall a fine vista awaits you. On the evening of July 2, the rugged heights in front were well secured by Union infantry and artillery. It is logical that this was where Hillyer's tired and depleted regiment would have realigned quickly for its final advance into Plum Run Valley.

To RESUME THE TOUR, from the stone wall, walk down into Plum Run Valley past the iron marker to Captain Smith's 4th New York Battery. Continue across Crawford Avenue and Plum Run, until you near the base of Little Round Top. At the base of the hill simply look up. In doing so, you may experience in some small way the impossibility of the task confronting Anderson's surviving soldiers as they approached this formidable position late on July 2. And surely, here is a good time to recall the words of Captain Hillyer as stated in his official report of the battle: "We found it to be the strongest natural position I ever saw."

FOR THE LAST LEG OF THE JOURNEY, return to the ridge and the little stone wall and again survey the scene. It was along this wall that Captain Hillyer and other officers of the brigade successfully rallied the troops of Anderson's command after their retreat from Little Round Top. The exhausted Georgians had just completed three hours of perilous combat, and yet as Hillyer explained, his soldiers were still all "well in hand," and had not lost their self-possession. When the 9th Georgia began the afternoon assault, there were 340 rank and file members of the regiment standing on Seminary Ridge prepared for the deadly work ahead. Along this stone wall, at 7 p.m., probably less than 80 of Hillyer's men were present to answer the next call of duty.

DEPENDING ON YOUR CHOICE OF RETURN ROUTES, remember that the Ninth Regiment, along with the remainder of Anderson's Brigade, moved back to Rose Run and went into bivouac for the night. There, the Georgians cared for the wounded of both sides, while attempting to rest and recuperate for what might come the following day. It was near that stream, during the long night, that Hillyer heard the soldier with the beautiful voice sing out his sadness and anguish at the terrible scenes around him. And on July 3, this was the area where James Norwood killed the Federal sharpshooter who was hidden behind the clay root.

* * *

This ends the core walking tour. If you are on foot, the easiest route back to the parking lot on Seminary Ridge is to follow Crawford Avenue to the left until you reach the Wheatfield Road. Then hike westward to the "Peach Orchard," and continue onto Millerstown Road and finally to the distant observation tower. You may, of course, also simply walk back across the "wheatfield" itself to Wheatfield Road, which will save time.

WHEN YOU ARRIVE AT THE PARKING LOT, there are three interesting places you may wish to visit by automobile that pertain to Captain Hillyer's experience at Gettysburg.

First are the sites associated with the 9th Georgia's activities on Friday, July 3, against Union cavalry forces. To visit these positions, leave the observation tower parking lot, and stay on West Confederate Avenue until you reach the Emmitsburg Road. Turn right, and drive about one half mile until you see a small stone and white frame building on the *right* side of the road. This was the Alexander Currens farmhouse, and the Ninth, in support of the other regiments of Anderson's Brigade, deployed here on the morning of July 3. Their disposition ran to the right and left of the house, facing south, toward the threat posed by Federal horsemen. Hillyer's regiment straddled the road itself.

At one critical point in this action, Hillyer detached his regiment from the line and marched his men back to the aid of a Confederate artillery unit. This movement took the 9th Georgia northward to assist the gunners of Bachman's Battery. To view that area, turn around and return to Confederate Avenue. At the intersection, go right onto the av-

This is likely a portion of the stone wall where the 9th Georgia assisted the 1st Texas.

enue and park at Benning's Brigade tablet just inside the woods. On the left of the road is an iron marker to Bachman's South Carolina Battery, and in the distance is the house and barn of the Bushman farm. From this overlook, one can take in much of the battlefield as described by Captain Hillyer. If you read the paragraphs associated with this skirmish, keep in mind that the Ninth eventually joined the 1st Texas Regiment at a "rock wall." That wall is located further down and traverses the avenue, just beyond the monument to "The Soldiers and Sailors of the Confederacy." The 1st Texas occupied the stone fence down below the ridge to the east, whereas the 9th Georgia likely held this upper section of the wall, or an area nearby. (Be forewarned: if you wish to visit this wall, it's a good idea to drive to the picnic area ahead, park, and then go on by foot, because the road becomes "one way" at that point.) You may recall that the rock wall was where Privates Rains and Upshaw bravely went out to recover the wounded Yankee cavalryman. There too, Captain Hillyer was complimented by Major Sellers, and ordered to return to the original line at the Currens house. The Ninth remained on the Currens farm until the close of the battle.

On several occasions in this book, the casualties of Anderson's Brigade have been discussed. As a final supplementary part of this tour, if you would like to see the farm where Hood's Division established its main field hospital, then turn around and return to the Emmitsburg Road. There, go to the right, and drive to the next intersection at the Millerstown Road. At the Millerstown Road, make a left and travel less than a mile to Black Horse Tavern Road. Here make a right turn, proceed to Willoughby Run Road, and bear right again. Shortly thereafter you will encounter a large privately operated farm complex. However, amidst all of these modern structures, the original house and barn of Sarah and John Edward Plank still stand. It was on this farm that General Hood's wounded (including Anderson's Brigade's casualties), were cared for. The hospital was in operation for about six weeks under the command of Surgeon F. A. Means, 11th Georgia Infantry. When General Lee began his withdrawal from Gettysburg, 515 men were left behind at this hospital, out of the division's 1300-1500 total wounded. In 1866, there were 64 identified Confederate graves (and 54 unknowns) still visible on the property, many of them buried "back of the barn," and "north of the house." Most of these human remains were returned to the South in the early 1870s.

John and Sarah Plank's farm was the field hospital for Hood's Division.

WE HOPE YOU HAVE ENJOYED following the memories and experiences of Captain Hillyer around the Gettysburg battlefield. Thank you for your participation on the tour, and your interest in his story. To return to town, either back track to the Emmitsburg Road, or stay on Willoughby Run Road until you reach the Fairfield Road. There, turn right, and Gettysburg is only about two miles away.

Notes

1. Captain Hillyer's battle account originally came from an address he delivered to a group of Confederate veterans in Walton County, Georgia, on August 2, 1904. His paper was subsequently published as a sixteen-page pamphlet by the Walton *Tribune*, entitled *Battle of Gettysburg*. In order to convert Captain Hillyer's address into a narrative booklet for the general public, his memoir has been edited to make his meaning clearer. The actual flow has been interrupted as little as possible. However, at times it was necessary to deviate somewhat from his original words and exact sentence structure. For the purist, the editor suggests a look at the original document as printed by the *Tribune*. There is currently one located in the archives of the University of Georgia at Athens. Hillyer's official report and the letter to his father were not edited except to add a first name or two. For a good general article on Anderson's Brigade during the battle of July 2, see "Anderson Attacks the Wheatfield," by Jay Jorgensen in *The Gettysburg Magazine*, # 14, January 1996, p. 64. And for the July 3 cavalry fight, see "The 1st Texas Infantry and the Repulse of Farnsworth's Charge," by Paul Shevchuk in *The Gettysburg Magazine*, # 2, January 1990, p. 81.

2. In February 1863, General James Longstreet, commander of the First Corps of the Army of Northern Virginia, was ordered to the Suffolk, Virginia area. With two of his divisions, Longstreet was directed by General Robert E. Lee to block any Union advance on Richmond from that quarter. Although some fighting did occur, when no real threat materialized, Longstreet turned the foray into a supply gathering expedition. His presence in that locale lasted well into May.

3. Besides General John B. Hood's Division of Alabama, Arkansas, Georgia and Texas troops, Longstreet took along General George E. Pickett's Division, which contained brigades from North Carolina and Virginia.

4. Captain George Hillyer belonged to Company C, 9th Georgia Infantry Regiment, of General George T. Anderson's Brigade, and General Hood's Division, of Lee's Army of Northern Virginia. Lee's Army was one of almost 20 Confederate field armies established during the war. Generally, a company consisted of about 100 men, a regiment, 1000 men, a brigade 5000 men, a division 15,000-25,000 men, and so on. But by 1863, due to casualties of one sort or another, all of these units were at one third their normal strength. For instance, the 9th Georgia fielded about 350 officers and men at Gettysburg. Anderson's Brigade took about 1800 soldiers into battle on July 2, while Hood's Division contained approximately 7500 on that same day.

5. General Lee's summer campaign into Maryland and Pennsylvania began on June 2, 1863. General Richard S. Ewell's Second Corps was in the advance, while General James E. B. Stuart's cavalry division guarded the Confederate army's right flank. It is believed that Lee's plan was to keep his men busy collecting supplies, in expectation that the Union's Army of the Potomac would move northward out of Virginia to protect their homes and countryside. Lee would then unite his three scattered army corps and the cavalry division, with the intent of fighting the Federals on ground of his own choosing. However, as we know, this strategy was interrupted by the unexpected collision of elements of the two armies near Gettysburg.

6. General Ewell was successful at Winchester and Stephenson's Depot, Virginia on June 13-15, where he defeated and captured a large part of General Robert H. Milroy's command, and took some greatly needed supplies.

7. Captain Hillyer's regiment, along with most of Longstreet's First Corps, arrived just west of Gettysburg and the battlefield early on July 2, traveling in along the Chambersburg-Cashtown-Gettysburg Turnpike, and crossing South Mountain. They went into bivouac for a few hours near Marsh Creek, and then moved to the vicinity and rear of Herr Ridge. Then just before one o'clock, McLaws's and Hood's Divisions began a march southeastward toward Seminary Ridge where they took final positions in preparation for Longstreet's assault against the Union army's left flank. This last halt put the brigade south of the Millerstown Road. Pickett's Division remained west of the mountain to guard the corps' supply wagons.

8. It is impossible to know exactly where Hillyer saw these officers, but the London correspondent was probably Francis Lawley, and the Prussian was Major Justus Scheibert. There is some confusion in the flow of Hillyer's account. He seems to indicate that his brigade marched to Seminary Ridge early on the morning of July 2, and then it traveled to the right along that ridge until its final position near the Troup Artillery. It is more likely that Longstreet's troops marched over from the Chambersburg Road to the area of Black Horse Tavern, then southward for a short distance more. There, a counter-march was ordered due to the sighting of a Union signal station on Little Round Top. The divisions then turned back up to the Fairfield Road and moved up and past the Adam Butt farm, then around to a lane along Willoughby Run, where eventually they reached Pitzer's School, almost a mile west of the "Peach Orchard." At the school, McLaws's men went east toward Seminary Ridge, and Hood's Division bypassed McLaws, ending up along the same ridge but further to the south.

9. Lieutenant Frederick Bliss of Company B, 8th Georgia, age 22, was a native of Savannah. He was shot on July 2, and died early on July 4 in the John Edward Plank farmhouse (Hood's Division field hospital), from the effects of the amputation of his right leg. Eventually Bliss's remains were recovered, and in February 1866 his mother Emma had them buried in Savannah's Laurel Grove Cemetery. Rev. Flynn was an army chaplain and a Presbyterian minister, but little else is known of him.

10. The Troup Artillery was formed in 1861 in LeGrange, Georgia. At Gettysburg they fought with H.C. Cabell's Battalion and suffered six casualties, including Captain Carlton who was wounded on July 3, plus 13 horses killed. Hillyer was mistaken about one thing here, for there were several more batteries in place to the right of the Troup Artillery.

11. On July 2 Longstreet was ordered by General Lee to attack the Union left flank which was located about two miles south of Gettysburg. General Longstreet was not in favor of this plan, and tried to convince Lee to alter his tactics. In the end, Longstreet set up his formation with Hood's Division on the right of the line, west and southwest of the Round Tops, and McLaws's Division on Hood's left. The attack began about four o'clock.

12. The "line officers" of a regiment were the captains and lieutenants; field officers were majors, lieutenant colonels, and colonels. Unlike Lieutenant Bliss, Private Giles's grave (if it too was at the Plank farm), was never identified. And if his remains were later recovered, their present location is unknown today.

13. Longstreet's two divisions were formed for the attack with the brigade of General Law on the far right, supported by Benning. Next, on Law's left was placed Robertson's Brigade, backed by General Anderson's troops. (Hillyer's own brigade). Then continuing the formation line were Generals Joseph Kershaw and William Barksdale, supported by the brigades of Paul Semmes and W. T. Wofford.

14. A "stake and rider" generally referred to a fence constructed of split rails surmounting a rock wall. However, the names used to describe fence styles used during the 19th Century varied in different parts of the country. Therefore, Hillyer could have meant that the fence where Stephens died was a "Virginia worm fence" or perhaps even a common "post and rail." As in the case of Private Giles, the grave of John F. Stephens, if properly marked, did not survive as an identified site. If his remains were recovered when the majority of the Confederate dead were removed from Gettysburg between 1871 and 1873, the location of his grave is presently unknown.

15. Captain Hillyer was correct. General McLaws's advance, for some curious reason, was held back. This caused a particular consternation in Anderson's ranks, because it allowed the Federals to concentrate their firepower on Hood's Division alone. At this stage of the attack, Captain Hillyer was given command of the regiment because Lieutenant Colonel John C. Mounger, Major William M. Jones, and senior Captain James M.D. King were either killed or wounded. The actual colonel of the Ninth in 1863 was Benjamin Beck, but he was not present due to a wound received in 1862 at Second Manassas.

Lieutenant William A. Tennille of Company D, 9th Georgia was eventually appointed captain, and, adjutant and inspector general on the staff of General Anderson. He was retired due to disease disability in January 1865.

Lieutenant John W. Arnold of Company C was wounded three times during the war, and was elected captain of Hillyer's old company on October 17, 1863. He was present at the surrender of the Army of Northern Virginia, April 9, 1865 at Appomattox C.H., Virginia.

16. Daniel N. Easley was elected second lieutenant in Company C June 13, 1861. He was wounded at Rappahannock Bridge, March 29, 1862, and later resigned his commission on March 25, 1864.

Evidently Private Ephrain Prince did not die behind that boulder. According to an earlier statement by Hillyer, and information contained in his military records, Prince was shot in both thighs and captured, and died in a U.S. field hospital near Gettysburg on July 17, 1863. Private Warrenton Rogers was likely killed outright as indicated by the captain. After the passage of 41 years, it was probably not always possible for Hillyer to exactly remember in detail all of the sights encountered during that confusing battle.

17. General Daniel Sickles, commander of the Third Corps of General George G. Meade's Army of the Potomac, was wounded in the leg by a cannon ball just west of Catherine Trostle's barn at about 5:30 p.m. on July 2. From all sources available, it appears that Sickles's horse did not run away when the general was helped to the ground after being struck with the projectile.

18. There are several accounts extant that describe the mortal wounding of General Semmes. One places him near a stone wall a little to the east of George and Dorothy Rose's stone farmhouse. This is a few hundred yards further to the west of where Hillyer saw him in the brook. The brook or stream is known today as Rose Run (an upper tributary of Plum Run), and was part of the runoff from Rose's spring. The spring-house was situated north of the main dwelling.

19. At this point in the story, Captain Hillyer is somewhat abbreviated when describing the movements of the brigade. He gives the impression that once the brigade moved from Rose Hill down the "declivity" into the meadow and stream-bed, it remained there until the general attack against Little Round Top. The fact is, sometime after the Union flanking party struck the left of the 9th Georgia, Anderson's

Brigade, after it moved down the hill, was forced to retire up the "declivity" about 200 yards, probably to a stone wall west of Rose Hill. Here it rallied, then charged again, but once more after a "fearful struggle" it was obliged to retreat. (This was the fight in the brook). The unit pulled itself together again, and made a third and final successful assault, along with Kershaw's and Wofford's Brigades, which drove the Federals out of the wheatfield area, and put the Confederates on a course toward Little Round Top.

In the July 2 fight, Anderson's Brigade consisted of four units, the 8th, 9th, 11th, and 59th Georgia Infantry Regiments. The 7th Georgia, also part of the brigade, was detached to guard against any Union attack on Longstreet's rear or flank. The total number of men carried into battle by those four regiments was about 1500. Their loss was 700. On that day, Anderson's men fought Northerners from the Union's Third, Second, and Fifth Army Corps. The Federal unit Hillyer described carrying the new battle flag may have been the 81st Pennsylvania of Colonel Edward Cross's brigade. James McHale was the color bearer. See Michael Dreese's book *Never Desert the Old Flag,* p.63.

20. The identity of the battery mentioned by Hillyer is not known, as the two artillery units in that area of the field, the 4th Battery, New York Light Artillery, and Battery D, 1st New York Light Artillery, did not show any guns lost to Anderson's Brigade.

    Little Round Top was approximately 650 feet above sea level, so it did rise about 150 to 200 feet above where Hillyer stood. There could have been as many as 12 guns on the hill, but not the number estimated by Captain Hillyer.

    Private James J. Mead enlisted into Company C on June 12, 1861. He was captured at Gettysburg on July 3, and was incarcerated in the U.S. military prison at Fort Delaware, Delaware, until his release on June 14, 1865. The battery Mead fired into could have been Battery L, 1st Ohio Light Artillery, or Battery D, 5th U.S. Artillery. The Zouave regiment was most likely the 155th Pennsylvania Infantry, a unit that had adopted the "Zouave" style of uniform.

    "Newn" Hudson has not been positively identified, but was probably Private William A. Hudson, who served in both Company D and K. He was captured near Spotsylvania Court House, Virginia, May 25, 1864, and sent to Fort Delaware until paroled in February 1865. James W. Morrow was then second lieutenant of Company H, 11th Georgia. He entered the service in July 1861, and was soon promoted to sergeant and then lieutenant. Morrow became a first lieutenant shortly after Gettysburg, and advanced to the rank of captain in March 1865. He was present at the Appomattox surrender the following month.

21. Major Henry D. McDaniel entered Confederate service as a lieutenant in Company H, 11th Georgia. He was promoted to captain in August 1862, and to major the following November, and held the position of quartermaster at various times during his career. McDaniel was wounded in the abdomen at Funkstown, Maryland on July 10, 1863, and captured at Hagerstown on July 12. He remained a prisoner of war at Johnson's Island, Ohio until July 25, 1865, and was elected governor of Georgia during the 1880s.

    The regiment that Hillyer speaks of here may have been the 110th Pennsylvania of Colonel Philippe Regis de Trobriand's Brigade. Today there is a monument to that unit in the general location noted by the captain.

22. Concerning the removal of casualties, most of the wounded from Anderson's Brigade were cared for at Hood's Division hospital on the Sarah and John E. Plank farm, located nearly two miles west-northwest of the battle area.

Curiously, a wounded soldier of the 64th New York reported that the "commander" of the 9th Georgia kindly assisted him and other disabled Union men during the night of July 2-3. That Northerner was Corporal William W. Moore of Company F. Moore also recalled that the unknown Confederate officer traded canteens and pocketknives with him. Whether or not the officer was Hillyer or not is impossible to know. See the *Report of the Seventh Annual Reunion of the 64th N.Y. Regimental Association at Salamanca, N.Y., Aug. 21-22, 1895...*pp. 56-59.

23. Private W. Calvin Thomas entered the service in 1861, was wounded at the Battle of Spotsylvania on May 12, 1864, and was present at Lee's surrender on April 9, 1865. So truly, as Captain Hillyer said, he did become "a fine soldier."

    The two Michael brothers spoken of by George Hillyer may have been Thomas, Starnes M., or Antoine. Antoine and Starnes enlisted in October 1862, and Thomas in February 1863. Of the three, Thomas did not survive the war, for he was mortally wounded at Gettysburg.

24. Captain Robert A. Hardee was the commander of Company H. He was wounded during the war, place unreported, and eventually resigned due to disability on March 1, 1863.

    Captain Hillyer seems to have known his men pretty well, and his memory of events has proven quite accurate. In the narrative Hillyer claims that one of the Norwood brothers, probably William E., was killed during the Suffolk campaign. However, William's short and incomplete military record states that he died of pneumonia on January 27, 1862. The second brother, James E., enlisted on June 6, 1861, and was wounded and captured at Lee's Mill, Virginia on February 14, 1865. James was discharged from a U.S. hospital in Washington, D.C. on August 8, 1865. Therefore, the reader will have to choose for William the fate that suits him best.

25. General Lee's right flank at Gettysburg was unprotected by cavalry, and therefore vulnerable to attack. Very early on July 3, Meade's cavalry chief, General Alfred Pleasonton, ordered General Judson Kilpatrick, with his Third Division of the Union Cavalry Corps, in conjunction with General Merritt's First Division Reserve Brigade, to move against the Confederate right and rear. The ensuing action proved a setback for the Federals, mainly due to the rough nature of the terrain (rock walls, thick woods, and rail fences), and the stubborn resistance offered by Southern infantrymen.

26. First Lieutenant Charles K. Maddox entered Confederate service in May 1861 as a sergeant, but was elected second lieutenant a year later. He was wounded at Gettysburg, and again on June 28, 1864. Maddox became a captain in January 1864, and was on detached duty in Georgia when the war ended. In the original text, Hillyer called Maddox "colonel," so he was either confused, or was using a postwar honorary title.

    William J. Hudson was the captain of Company I, 7th Georgia, and was wounded three times during the war. He was present at Appomattox when the end came, April 9, 1865.

    Captain William A. Bachman's battery was know as the *German Light Artillery*, and was raised in Charleston, South Carolina in the spring of 1862. On July 2 it was fighting with Major M. W. Henry's Artillery Battalion of Longstreet's First Corps.

    Lieutenant Arnold, as noted in note # 15 above, took command of Company C when Hillyer was ordered to lead the regiment on July 2.

Captain Robert K. Holliday appears to have been the regimental quartermaster of the 7th Georgia in 1863, but officially, he became General Anderson's assistant brigade quartermaster on September 15, 1864.

All "company grade" or *line* officers led their men on foot, but regimental and staff officers were mounted. Therefore, when Hillyer took command of the 9th Georgia, he was entitled to the use of a horse.

Twenty-five year old General Elon J. Farnsworth commanded the First Brigade of Kilpatrick's Third Cavalry Division, consisting of New York, Pennsylvania, Vermont, and West Virginia troops. He was killed in combat on July 3, and some historians believe that a rash charge ordered by Kilpatrick was the cause. This attack was made over rough terrain against Confederate infantry and had little chance of success. Farnsworth's loss was 21 killed, 34 wounded, and 43 captured. For more on Captain George Hillyer's experiences that day, see the address he gave at the Gettysburg monument dedication for the First Vermont Cavalry, at: http://vermontcivilwar.org/1cav/h/119.shtml

27. Private Littleton R. Raines joined the 9th Georgia as a private on March 4, 1862 and was killed in battle near Knoxville, Tennessee November 29, 1863.

    Private Robert A. Upshaw entered the C. S. Army in June 1861, and his military record reports he was wounded at Gettysburg on July 2. He was still in the ranks at Appomattox, April 9, 1865.

    The wall in question generally runs a couple of hundred yards east and west and up over Seminary Ridge. There it connects to a wall on the crest that is aligned basically north and south.

28. William H. Sellers, with the rank of captain and then major, served on the staff of General Hood as assistant adjutant general from March 19, 1862 through December 1863. He was promoted to lieutenant colonel in early 1865, and assigned to General R. E. Lee's staff in the same capacity until the end of the war.

    The losses of the 8th Georgia were 168 men killed, wounded, and missing; the 9th Georgia's total casualties were 189. (34 killed, 123 wounded, and 32 missing). The percentage of loss for the Eight was 53.8, and for the Ninth, 55.6. The highest percent loss in Pickett's Division was in the 8th Virginia with 92.2, followed closely by the 18th Virginia at 78.5. Most of the other thirteen regiments of Pickett's Division suffered casualties nearer to the numbers of the 9th Georgia. However, Hillyer was correct if we use only the figure for the *killed and wounded,* because a very large number of Pickett's losses were due to men captured by the enemy.

29. For a complete account of Lieutenant Colonel Mounger's death and burial, see my 2001 book, *Confederates Killed in Action at Gettysburg,* p. 83. By the end of the war, Mounger's wife had lost her husband and three sons killed in battle. Captain King died in the U.S military prison at Johnson's Island, Ohio on November 4, 1863, and is buried in the camp cemetery. Major William Jones, age 24, died of wounds received at Spotsylvania on May 12, 1864. He is buried in Hollywood Cemetery, Richmond. E. W. Bowen of Company I, who was killed on July 2, entered the service as a private in June 1861, and was elected second lieutenant in 1863.

    For the exact casualties of the 9th Georgia, see note # 28 above. The "detailed statement of casualties" mentioned by Hillyer has never been found.

30. The action Captain Hillyer describes in the first part of the letter took place during Lee's retreat near Funkstown, Maryland, a village just southeast of Hagerstown on the Boonsboro road. This area was the left flank of Lee's rear guard, or main

line of battle, and General Stuart used his cavalry and some infantry to repulse an enemy advance there on July 10.

Corporal William G. Raines was wounded on July 2, and later killed in action at Knoxville, Tennessee December 18, 1863. Private Jasper McGauhey was wounded and captured on July 10 at Funkstown, Maryland. He was cared for at the Seminary Hospital in Hagerstown, Maryland, and is thought to have remained a prisoner of the Federals until the end of the war. The identity of "Capt. Scott" is not known. Lieutenant Arnold is mentioned in note # 15. Lieutenant Early is possibly W.H. Early, who was an officer in Cobb's Georgia Legion of General Wofford's Brigade. Lieutenant Morrow is identified in note # 20, and Private Anderson W. Reese was a relative of Hillyer's serving in the Troup Artillery. The cousin was Francis L. Hillyer, a first lieutenant in Company C, 3rd Georgia Infantry. He did survive Gettysburg, but twelve days later was killed in the fighting at Manassas Gap, Virginia. See note # 21 for more on Major McDaniel's record.

Captain John D. Webb of Company D enlisted at that rank in 1861. He was wounded in the left arm at Ream's Station, Virginia on August 25, 1864, and the arm was amputated at the shoulder joint. Webb was elected major of the Ninth on October 26, 1864 and lieutenant colonel on February 23, 1865.

Jackson Giles fate is covered in note # 12.

Private Warrenton Rogers was killed on July 2. He had enlisted into Company C on June 13, 1861. Thomas L. B. Atkinson, who was also killed July 2, joined Company C as a private on March 4, 1862. Private John F. Stephens enlisted on June 13, 1861 and died at Gettysburg July 2. (See note # 14) Private Cornelius H. Ragan came to Hillyer's company March 4, 1862, and was killed in action July 2. See note # 16 for private Ephrain Prince's record. "Jack" McDaniel has not been successfully identified. Private William S. Brown of Company C, was wounded at Savage Station, Virginia on June 29, 1862, and was captured near Gettysburg on July 2. Brown was confined at Point Lookout prison in Maryland until February 22, 1864, when he enlisted into U.S. service. Private John B. Perkins, also of Company C, was captured at Gettysburg on July 2, and did not go over to the Federals. Instead, he stayed true to his comrades, bur remained a prisoner at Elmira, New York until June 14, 1865. Private James W. Conner, another Company C veteran, was indeed captured on July 2 at Gettysburg, and was sent to the military prison at Point Lookout, Maryland until exchanged at James River, Virginia on February 20, 1865. Wilson Woodruff was probably Private James W. Woodruff of Company C, who was captured on July 2, and sent to Fort Delaware prison in Delaware, until exchanged at James River, Virginia on March 10, 1865.

31. The sources for the biographical sketch of George Hillyer came partly from his service records in the National Archives, but mainly from material kindly provided by Bernard W. Wolff of Roswell, Georgia and by Mary Robinson and Brion FitzGerald of Fairfield, Pennsylvania. Judge Hillyer's obituary is from the October 4, 1927 Atlanta *Constitution,* and was supplied by Charlotte Ray of Atlanta. The quote concerning Private Sampson Sill is from the Internet site of *The Ninth Georgia Infantry, CSA,* while the 1904 veterans quote is from the address cited in note # 1.

Note: For those interested in reading another Gettysburg Campaign report concerning the 9th Georgia, see the Internet web site for the Ninth Georgia Infantry: http://members.aol.com/Treygriffn/index133.html. It contains a letter written July 22, 1863 and signed by "G," published in the August 11 edition of *The Confederate Union* of Milledgeville, Georgia. Much of this account covers the July 2 death of Lieutenant Colonel John C. Mounger, and some researchers are convinced that Captain Hillyer was the author.

Greg Coco speaking with servicemen in the Gettysburg National Military Park Soldiers' National Cemetery on July 19, 2005 *(Katie Lawhon, NPS)*.

About the Author

Gregory Ashton Coco, born and raised in Louisiana, lived in the Gettysburg area for nearly 35 years.

In 1972, after serving in the U.S. Army, he earned a degree in American History from the University of Southwestern Louisiana. While in the military, Greg spent a tour of duty in Vietnam as a prisoner of war military interrogator and infantry platoon radio operator with the 25th Infantry and received, among other awards, the Purple Heart and Bronze Star.

During his years in Gettysburg, Greg worked as a National Park Service Ranger and a Licensed Battlefield Guide. He wrote sixteen books and a dozen scholarly articles on Gettysburg and the Civil War. His book *A Strange and Blighted Land. Gettysburg: The Aftermath of a Battle* was voted #12 in the Top 50 Civil War Books ever written.

Greg died at age 62 in February of 2009. In his words, he was "the happy husband of Cindy L. Small for 26 years. He was the fortunate father of daughter Keri E. Coco. He loved them both with all his heart." Keri is married to Cail MacLean and they have a daughter, Ashton MacLean Coco.